FOOD, FAITH & FACING MY FEARS

A memoir

PATIENCE DORMAN

"Therefore I tell you, do not worry about your life, what you will eat or drink; or about your body, what you will wear. Is not life more important than food and the body more important than clothes? Look at the birds in the air; they do not sow or reap or store away in barns, and yet your heavenly Father feeds them. Are you not much more valuable than they?" Matthew 7:25-26

INTRODUCTION:

TAKING A STEP BACK

I always have pictured my life as a series of phases. Ones of hanging out with certain people, doing certain things, or thinking a certain way. By the time I'm 90 years old and sitting on my deathbed, I expect to own a device that enables me to stream brief summaries of each phase through the screen of my iPhone (or whatever device we're using then).

As I reflect on my past, I can never seem to grasp when the switch between phases flipped. Never have I awakened with a different set of friends, a brand new body, or an altered view of the world, but when I think about who I am today, so many of my already-written chapters seem fictitious. They all seep into each other like a watercolor painting. My eighteen years have been a continuous stream of changes and different versions of myself. Ultimately, they compose the masterpiece I title, "Life."

PART I:

FOOD

CHAPTER 1:

BEGINNINGS

Health has been instilled in me for as long as I can remember. Growing up, my mom cooked meals at home for my sisters, dad, and I almost every night. We'd eat as a family at our screechy oak table. My sisters (Sammy and Mille) and I learned that it's important to eat our fruits and vegetables, but don't let me fool you. My parents could care less about being "organic" or enforcing special diets. Although we were never prohibited from eating certain foods, we simply saw the lack of soda and potato chips in our house as an unarguable fact. Cake, Captain Crunch, and Chinese takeout were for special occasions. Birthdays, the Super Bowl, and dance recitals had a whole new element of delight because of the decadent food that tagged along.

Although I was later thankful for this lifestyle my parents infringed on me, my ten-year-old self, inevitably, yearned for what I didn't get at home. I'd sleepover with friends whose pantries were stocked with my wildest dreams: Pop Tarts, Oatmeal Creme Pies, and Capri-Suns, all within reach at any moment. Getting to devour pre-packaged snacks with my friends became a euphoric joy. We'd bake the only thing we knew how—Pillsbury Ready-to-Bake Cookies, then devour them over innocent giggles and America's Next Top Model. Sleepovers justified a kind of indulging on food that I didn't normally experience and I loved it. Little did I know, the gears between my emotions and food were slowly starting to grind.

My parents raised my sisters and I relaxed and independently. Unlike many families in town, they didn't force us into sports; rather, they encouraged us to do what we liked. This included singing, dancing, drawing, and most commonly, playing Barbies for hours on end. Miraculously, my parents still managed to get us involved in the community. The Dorman girls were always present at play dates, parades, and vacation bible schools around town.

I tried some sports, but the only ones I kept with were swim and dance. Because of this, my competitive edge became lesser than that of my peers. I'd opt out of physical hardships for more creative pastimes, such as writing and art—I was the girl making dandelion necklaces on the sidelines of my soccer game. I'd walk to school, ride my bike, and play freeze tag, but nothing physical was ever taken too seriously. That was just the way I liked it.

In middle school, I, predictably, sported the title of "picked last in gym class." Even when I gave it a try in matt ball, all I could think when it was my turn to hit the ball was: *this is hell.* I would have much rather been in art, lunch, or even math class. This put my pre-puberty self in an uncomfortable, uncoordinated funk. Those days, sports were *the* outlet to popularity. There was no swim team at my school, and dance automatically designated me as a, God forbid, "girly-girl." Despite the fact that I physically had no hope, I'd beg my mom to buy me shin guards and cleats so I could fit in.

Peer pressure swooped in, and I tried some team sports. I attempted to survive and pretended to be entertained in games with kids who were probably cradled to sleep by the sweet sounds of ESPN. The truth, that I wouldn't dare expose, was that running around on the soccer field or basketball court wasn't my idea of a fun time. I would have much rather been writing the newest chapter in my juicy, pre-teen novel or learning how to do my makeup via pretty girls on Youtube.

CHAPTER 2:

HIGH SCHOOL, HIGHLIGHTS,

HIGH HOPES

High school was a breath of fresh air. Unlike middle school, every kid didn't play every sport—more importantly not every *popular* kid played every sport. I gained confidence, maybe even relief, that I could quit pretending for the sake of inclusion. I could be involved and interact with others by simply being social. I submerged myself in student government, art, work, and a bubbling social life.

My mom ran, and still runs, recreationally, and my sister ran for the high school cross country team. Although I couldn't see how running 3.1 miles against others could be *fun,* I also wanted to be involved in *something*. I assessed the pros of the situation: no matter how good I was, I'd still get the glory of just being an athlete. More importantly, I could come in last place and it wouldn't be *completely* mortifying because no one (well, at least no one cool) went to cross country meets anyways. After plenty of persuasion and reminders that "it's not taken seriously," I joined my high school cross country team.

Our coach was a young, tall marathon runner, and our team was composed of about ten kids total —that is, everyone was on varsity. The sport's allure included five mile runs in Missouri's humidity, intensive interval training, and meets where I got passed by girls who likely came running out of their mother's wombs.

I managed to keep up with the team at practice, but when a meet came around, the voice in my head never failed to cry: *I'm going to die. I am going to die right here at the two mile marker.*

Needless to say, I hated running. But I kept with it because, even if I never broke any records, I was still a freshman getting a varsity letter. Even if my legs felt like they might fall off, I still got to sit on the cross country float in the Homecoming Parade. People were impressed with me for simply doing the sport, and that was enough to satisfy me. I had somewhere to belong—better yet, I belonged somewhere it didn't matter if I was *actually* good.

I had yet to figure out that there was another perk to the sport, something that later became my only motivation to run; cross country got me in shape. My first year, I was having too grand of a time reaping the social benefits of being on a high school athletic team to actually think about my health. Besides, I had been tall and slender my whole life. As a freshman, my body wasn't something I dwelled on.

I still remember having butterflies in my stomach and quivers in my fingers the entire first week of high school. I felt like it was finally my opportunity to prosper and I was not going to mess that up. *Move over, 14 year old cigarette-smokers and dress-code violators, it's my time to shine!* I got my first boyfriend, had my first kiss (which I claimed was my second), and finished my first beer.

I loved being around all the older people, but I was well aware of my place at the bottom of the high school totem pole. I nestled myself in a niche of innocence, but flirted with dreams of *real* popularity. Every superficial rule that the older people in high school implied, I precisely followed.

CHAPTER 3:

A SEED IS PLANTED

Sophomore year saw me in a different light. No longer was I senior Sammy Dorman's freshman sister, but was now a social prodigy who underwent a beautiful strike of luck with puberty over the summer. My boobs had swelled up and I decided that my hair was meant to be blonde. I started dating and hanging out with older classmates. I could adapt and become friends with anyone I set my mind to. I was eager to take whatever activity the "cool" people were doing and show them up.

As my social status increased, so did the pressures I felt to fit in. I wanted boys to notice me; I wanted girls to want to be friends with me; I wanted, above all, to be the best. I claimed a "chill girl" character and did everything I possibly could to make that seem true. I strived to not be the nagging, annoying type of girl that everyone complained about. After mastering this, I could hang out with a room full of guys, drink like a champ, go to prom with The Seniors, and—with my closest friends by my side—grow up way too fast.

But reality always returned, crashing down on me with curfews and parental conflicts. Sophomore year my mom and I fought more than we have in all other phases combined. I couldn't quite fulfill my fantasy of being "down for anything" with her 11:00 curfews and harsh judgement of my peers. *Can't she see I have a reputation to build?!*

My group of friends was, and still is, composed of an array of larger-than-life personalities. This includes the vulgar comedian and multiple sport All-Stars. I accepted the fact that I would never be the funniest, smartest, or most athletic, so I turned to the only thing I knew I had for sure: my looks. I felt like my addition to the group's value was an unspoken title of the outgoing, pretty one. I thought my identity and any status I had relied solely on my appearance.

Desperate to find something that set me apart from others, I became convinced that my face, body, and hair would have to be the things to do it. As a fifteen year old in a tiny, conservative town, I still think this theory rang a bit of truth.

Despite my body image being more and more valued by others, I didn't think much about my nutrition or my well being (or my morals, for that matter). That, in combination with a new license to swing by Taco Bell whenever I pleased, led me to weigh heavier than I ever had before. My "dealing" with this was simply blowing my money on a bigger size of Guess Jeans and Victoria's Secret Yoga Pants.

I still ran, still had a pantry full of healthy foods, and still maintained a normal weight. My social life and my love handles were bulging over, but I was by no means overweight.

At first, I acted like my weight gain didn't bother me, but it was a growing source of irritation. There were few clothes from the year before that I could still squeeze into without them clinging on my stomach. People would tell me I was "starting to fill out," or was "getting thick." I'd commit myself to their words, regardless if they meant to compliment or criticize me. I read magazines, scrolled through Twitter, and went to the *cool* parties; I surrounded myself with slim, beautiful bodies. I noticed how much they seemed to have their life together. *If only I could do that...* The world around me was slowly but surely making me uncomfortably and meticulously aware of my fleshy figure.

Toward the end of my sophomore year, I realized I could take control. I realized that I could manipulate my body and make it look "good"— that I didn't have to be unhappy with myself. The imaginary link between my body and my consumption was emplaced in my radical, all-or-nothing mind, and it was monumental.

I began skipping lunch and limiting my food choices. I did some research but assumed I already knew which foods were "good" and which were "bad." I made lists of the food I consumed daily and when I, inevitably, chose something that wasn't under my realm of "healthy," it got a frowny-face emoji placed next to it. My daily goal was to keep the list small and to get no frowny-faces. Most of the time, I failed.

Moderation was not a word in my dictionary. I would cut out the bad stuff, cold turkey, only to end the day filled with desperation and a pint of Cookies-and-Cream ice cream in my stomach. At sixteen, I was already beginning to tumble down the corrupt slope that most dieters go down.

I'd create rules for myself, accidentally break them, then feel guilty because of my "lack of self-discipline." The restrictions I placed on myself enabled monotonous and shameful internal dialogue: *I'll start over tomorrow*, or *just this once*, or *Igiveupgivemethreeplatesofspagettiwithasideofpizza*, were common.

My view of exercise morphed from fun or social involvement into a way of tailoring my appearance. I gained a new, different infatuation for cross country. Running miles on end could help me perfect my body—*I guess it doesn't **totally** suck!* In the spring, I also played soccer, a sport that I had no interest in. This was partially motivated by the fact that all my friends played, but mostly due to my aim of getting in better shape.

My attempts to restrict myself from bread, pasta, and every single dessert were often forfeited by a fear of not fitting in or by a mean hunger to binge. I chastised myself for not following my set guidelines, but for the most part, I was still more entertained by my newly-established popularity.

Life continued and I eventually got comfortable with my mediocre ability to conquer personal goals and meet self-standards. I was not the skinniest, strongest, or most productive person, but I was okay with that because socially, I thrived. I hung out with friends, went to parties, went on dates, and established my niche in the status quo. I didn't think too deeply about much, and I reflected on my well-being about as much as I medaled in cross country meets—little to never.

My personal aspirations were secondary to other's recognition. I let the world impact me so much that I began to measure my worth by how much people liked me. I spent all my money on the newest, cutest clothes and name brand makeup. The superficial principles of media, high school, and society in general muffled what my subconscious so desperately wanted me to hear. Society's arbitrary rules were my sacred writ, and I became a victim of its body-image pressures.

Despite my social life taking off, feelings of discontent always came back at the end of the day. The voice in my head reminded me that if I just focused a little more, I would lose some weight and then I'd *really* have the whole package. I was convinced that all my problems would melt away if I could just melt off my fat first. I told myself that I was just on the edge of the ideal body and dreamed about what it would be like to actually achieve it.

I checked my stomach in the mirror daily and took selfies in my sports bra throughout the year to examine if I had made any progress in my pursuit of "perfection." I noticed when my circumference narrowed an inch, when I used the innermost clasp on my bra, and when the muscle in my forearm was visible. When I recognized these microscopic changes, my inner-critic would congratulate me; *keep at it girlfriend!*

Despite the inconsistency of my workouts and voluntary periods of starvation, by the time summer came around, I actually had made a little progress. *The calorie counting and boring soccer practices had actually paid off!* I was slightly more toned and, although no one else could tell, I saw a difference. That recognition alone was enough to catalyze my behavior for the next two years…

CHAPTER 4:

FINALLY

January of my junior year, my mom started a weight-loss challenge at the YMCA. It mimicked the famous TV show "Biggest Loser" and everyone in the community seemed to somehow be involved. I saw this contest as my opportunity to finally make some changes. I had already achieved my dreams of popularity and was settling into high school's hierarchy—bettering myself was my next goal.

Since middle school, I'd been busy meeting others' expectations; it was finally time to meet the expectations I had for myself. I was ready to listen to the little voice pestering me in the back of my head saying, *you can be better.* At the last minute, I joined a team to satisfy my high self-standards and to "gain control of my life." It was time to focus my strong drive on the thing I had wanted for so long.

I ensured everyone that I wasn't joining the contest to lose weight—and this was the truth! I didn't care about a silly number on a scale decreasing. I claimed to be motivated solely by the mental clarity that healthy eating and exercise brought me. I wanted the program to hold me accountable for my actions. I soon realized that I didn't care about what I actually weighed, but that I *did* care about how I looked. I secretly longed to lose my arm flab, ditch the cellulite and, just maybe, build a six pack.

The contest began, my blinders went on, and I was sprinting to the finish line. I immersed myself in research, books, and podcasts on everything health related. My motivation and productivity skyrocketed. I became the queen of healthy habits and nothing could disrupt my reign. I realized that this concept of "health" I'd been ever-striving for could be instilled with just a bit of self discipline.

Exercise, nutritious meals, and self-improvement practices became daily priorities. My routine began with a 5:00 a.m. High Intensity Interval Training class where I was easily the only person who still had seven hours of school and three hours of work to attend after.

Every morning, I made a smoothie out of protein powder, a frozen banana, powdered peanut butter, and greek yogurt—a mere 150 calories. These smoothies were my holy grail; I didn't want to consume anything else. After my H.I.I.T. class, I'd cut out an extra thirty minutes in my morning to ensure my precious smoothie and hot black coffee were enjoyed to their fullest extent. I'd wake up my sisters by blending my concoction and, as I headed out of the door, there was never a speck of the cold banana goodness left.

If we didn't have one of the ingredients, I was sickened with the anxiety of having to choose what else I could—would—eat. Cheerios, french toast, and Sammy's breakfast casserole were no longer options.

Mornings became my favorite time of day. There were no questions or uncertainty about how they would pan out. There was no external voice to bring me out of my satisfying ritual. I placed my comfort and security in that breakfast regimen and any alternative—waking up late, Mom making pancakes, early morning student government meetings—obliterated that.

After accepting any social shaming that came with skipping lunch at school, I forced myself to wait until I deemed it late enough in the evening to carefully craft a low-calorie dinner. As if my schedule wasn't packed enough with extracurricular activities, work, and communal events, I nudged runs on the trail in my backyard and miles on the elliptical at The Y into any spare second.

Working out became an everyday necessity and the first aspect of my life to suffer was, inevitably, my social life. No longer was the idea of popularity the wind behind my wings—my *personal* goals were now the supreme dictators of my behavior. I already had good friends and an established status. I excused myself from basketball games, movie nights, and brunch with girlfriends if they dared to interfere with my new, sanctified fundamentals.

Every push-up, set of stairs, and drop of sweat left me wanting more. I'd run two miles on the treadmill, feel unaccomplished and, therefore, completely unsatisfied. I would glance around the gym, overwhelmed by the decision of which machine to use next. While on seated rower, I'd think to myself, *I should probably do the bicep curler, too*. I'd haphazardly lift weights then go home and do an ab workout before I ate dinner. I couldn't go to sleep until I completed the amount of fitness that I considered adequate, even if that meant doing crunches on my floor when I got home from a party at midnight.

I heard that the "healthiest" way to eat was with many small meals throughout the day, but as much as I wanted, I couldn't execute this. I couldn't snack because I feared that any trial would lead to a ferocious binge which would later plague me with guilt. My black and white personality motivated my behavior and I swore that I would accomplish nothing with a middling demeanor. *Mediocrity will not aid the road to my dreams.*

I played games with myself to see how long I could go without eating. I discovered that the more regularly I skipped meals, the more numb I was to hunger. When the chef at my job asked me to try their "Soup du jour" I would a take spoonful, discretely spit it out, then boast about how fabulous it was. In a peculiar, sickening way, I began to prefer the feeling of hunger over fullness. A single Goldfish or Ritz cracker would throw off my day's course. Any calories were bad calories and contaminated my speckless day. My self-compassion was reliant on my self-deprivation.

I wrote down what I ate every day in my little turquoise planner. I started making my own meals and finding substitutes for high-calorie ingredients: protein powder as flour, lettuce as bread, avocado as butter. I experimented with seasoning and sauces to add flavor to the naturally bland, but (seemingly) nutritious dishes.

Given the rare occasion I went out to eat, I secretly wished it wouldn't be weird for me to ask the server to hold the cheese and bacon on my Chef's Salad.

A month later, it was time for the first weigh in for "The Biggest Loser." I was nervous. I could feel that I'd lost weight but had no relative range of how much. I was afraid the number might be bigger than expected and, while I was fine with that, I didn't want it to be publicized. Regardless, with my mom's eyes peering over my shoulder, I stepped on the scale. We looked down to see a number that I hadn't seen since my freshman year. A few hours later, they calculated the contestants' changes and, to everyone's surprise, I had the largest body mass index difference out of any one else in the contest. I had won. *What?!* I had lost ten pounds in a month.

CHAPTER 5:

SHORT LIVED PRIDE

I hadn't changed much physically, but my mindset was altered. I knew that ten pounds in a month was a bit extreme for my slim body, but overall, I didn't care about the number because I was filled with pride for the power I gained over myself. I felt as though I'd unlocked the secrets of health that everyone else desired.

Years before, I was accustomed to the idea that I would never be the best at anything, especially physical endeavors. Because of this, no prize could have compared to the heavy, gold medal of empowerment that I got after winning the contest. I had discovered my potential that, for years, I didn't think I had in me.

This transformed my thinking. I achieved my goals without the help of a mentor, a friend, or a hundred dollars. I felt so sure of the fact that I could do anything with the right mindset. I swelled with optimism, pride, and a radiating sense of self.

I was inspired to learn. I was inspired to work hard, to push myself, and to discover my full capability in everything. I dove deeply into the psychology behind food, exercise, and decision making in general. I realized that I could simply train my brain to derive pleasure from things I didn't like before. I had a theory that became my creed...

What's the difference between an apple and a cupcake? Cupcakes taste better because we, as a society, have grown to connect their sweet flavor to rewards and celebration. Digging deeper, we relate rewards and celebration to our sense of value, achievement, and belonging. In contrast, we're taught that 'an apple a day keeps the doctor away.' We're trained to think that fruit is healthy and that we HAVE to eat it or we'll be sick and fat. Of course people are going to resist what they feel like they are forced to eat! Society revolutionized our taste buds to prefer poor-quality, high-calorie foods over real, healthful food!

A switch in me had flipped; tasks that I used to despise like studying, cooking, running, and planning, started to become a source of comfort and thrill in my life. If I completed a full to-do list of clean eating, exercising, and micromanaging, my inner critic gave me a pat on the back. I experimented with mindful eating, meditation, and, naturally, the newest exercise or diet fad. I was willing to try anything if it would help me better myself.

With my newfound worship of productivity, I discovered the perfect job. I spent my weekends serving tables at The Fred, a local fine-dining restaurant located in a historic, boutique hotel. I landed the job just months before, in November, and was loving the quick cash, the excitement of a busy night, and getting to bond with all types of characters.

I was always moving: filling up drinks, resetting tables, or delivering trays full of of medium rare Ribeye steaks. When I served my regulars, the retired travelers, or the last-minute "let's go here"-ers, I could feel my personality blossom. I loved engaging with people and getting to make their experience at the restaurant just as delicious as their food. I loved introducing myself and, in return, getting "Patience" puns for the rest of the night. I loved the fact that when I had other people to care for, I wasn't thinking about food.

Working as a waitress also fueled a new fetish of being around food that I had unconsciously developed. The restaurant industry saw food the same way I did—it wasn't simply *fuel*—food, and the manipulation of it, was imperative. It was always being talked about, handled, and perfected. I was probably thinking about food just as much as our head chef, but in a totally different way. The Fred became another way to put my willpower to the test, a way to experience—to smell, see, and *obsess* over—food without breaking my commitment of not tasting it

I would go into work at 4:00 p.m. and test my hunger's endurance so that when I got off at nine, I could make my own nutritious meal. I was beginning to love and master both of my new occupations: waitressing and self-controlling.

CHAPTER 6:

BUSINESS OF BYSTANDERS

Since the program was community-wide and because I was quite the social butterfly, I received recognition for winning the first leg of the contest. "Where did you shed ten pounds from?" and "why would *you* need to lose weight?" were common. I never knew how to reply. I felt awkward, especially when my peers or teachers at school brought it up.

Some people told me that they were proud or impressed, but most commentary was negative. Despite this, I still obtained a sense of dignity. I truly believed that most of the people who commented were really just jealous that a sixteen-year-old girl could shave off ten pounds when they could not. Blame society, the media, or just my community, but I was under the impression that a good body was all that *anyone* ever wanted. I wanted everyone to know that if they could just realize the same things I had, then they *too* could lose weight! It never occurred to me that people might *actually* be happy just the way they were.

I noticed skinny people whose diets were composed of Snickers, Mountain Dew, and Doritos. While I was a bit jealous of their freedom, I knew my body simply did not operate that way. It especially annoyed me when people mentioned how "lucky" I was to have a good body. I would get flustered—*Hello! I am not sitting here, gorging on Girl Scout Cookies and diet soda! I worked my ass off for this!* I had dedicated every atom of my energy into perfecting my body. My toned figure was my greatest achievement and it was *not* to be regarded as some natural, God-given gift.

I became a firm believer that hard work delivers results, as if all my other goals (financial, academic, social) were now attainable with a simple change of mindset. I felt like Wonder Woman, summoning power in everything.

After a slew of comments said to her, my mom's short-lived pride in me died and she developed her own concerns. She told me, *as if I didn't already know*, that I was done with the contest. I would not be continuing to the Challenge's second month. This didn't bother me, though, because I learned that I did not need some piddly program to hold me accountable.

Adopting "health" and losing weight was a totally different ball game for me than it was for the middle-aged adults whom I was against. While they struggled through the month, for me, it was merely a challenge that I could—*would*—overcome. The lifestyle that gave me a sense of purpose. I got the first, tempting taste of the thing that my subconscious mind had been craving for years: *control*.

CHAPTER 7

CHICAGO

(WITHOUT THE DEEP DISH PIZZA)

I was going on my first big trip by myself. My aunt had a conference at a frilly hotel in downtown Chicago and I would ride a MegaBus to meet her there. After completing my morning workout and engulfing my smoothie, I was set to leave for my eight hour trip. I packed a single plastic bag of dried cranberries, almonds, and carrots, as well as a a mini granola bar to hold me over. I wanted to challenge myself, to reach a whole new level of willpower, and I planned to do it on this trip.

As I went about trying to sleep or read my book on the bus, I felt my snacks inflaming my every thought. The voice in my head reminded me that it was too early to eat my pretentious snacks. Eventually, the lack of the sustainment from my smoothie turned the almonds into eyes that wouldn't stop glaring at me. Soon, I reluctantly ripped open the bar, delved into the bag, and in a matter of seconds, my precious treats were gone. The hunger I still felt was muffled by an internal voice shaming me for not having enough self-control to postpone eating.

Around dinner time, the MegaBus stopped at a gas station for passengers to get food. I hopped off with all of my new Chicago-bound comrades. (Just kidding, nobody talked to each other the entire time.) I spent the whole prior hour contemplating whether or not I'd grant myself the indulgence of buying something to eat and I concluded that I wouldn't; I knew that no snack could make up for the guilt I'd feel after eating it.

Since I had already decided I would wait until I arrived in Chicago to eat, I walked into the Grub-and-Go with a blanket of assurance wrapped around me—I wasn't going to collapse at the site of food. As the other passengers got sub sandwiches and mocha frappes to endure the remainder of the trip, I looked around, appalled and slightly disgusted that anyone would choose such poor nourishment. *Does he know that his "healthy" snack is literally sugar coated with sugar?* I walked through the aisles and examined all the food. *Does she know that's not actually "low-fat"?*

I couldn't fathom the neglect of health consciousness around me. I looked at the Little Debbie snacks and promised myself I'd never let one of them contaminate my body ever again. Come to think of it, even if I did allow myself to purchase an item, there was nothing there that I would have considered worthy.

I finally arrived in Chicago; the city of beautiful architecture, deep dish pizza, and, at this time, below zero temperatures. After being dumped in downtown Chicago, I caught a taxi to the hotel that held my aunt's conference. She told me she'd grab me a plate of dinner from the meeting and meet me in the room. I wished I could have made my own plate with the choices and portions I pleased, but I didn't object, as my hunger had morphed into a wild roar.

We reunited and hugged. Then she left left me with my dinner because she had to go back to her meeting for a while. I sat alone in the lavish hotel room with a ravenous hunger and a plate of buffet-quality food. I devoured the salad and pork chop, then pushed around and contemplated eating the potatoes—they border-lined my standards.

As for the dinner roll, there was no contemplation. I had barely touched bread since "The Biggest Loser" and I knew I would later chastise myself if I indulged. *It's not worth it*, I reminded myself, *I won't eat it*. I laid my head back on the crisp white bedding and clicked on the TV. I was proud; the anxiety of questioning whether or not I could eat a roll was non-existent.

I tried to focus on the show in front of me, but there sat the roll, daunting me—its warm, golden skin glistening with melted butter. After a few minutes, I couldn't bear for it to lie in front of me for another second, so I destroyed it. I ripped it up, wrapped it in toilet paper, and put it in the porcelain toilet of the fancy hotel bathroom.

I knew my behavior was irrational and ridiculous, but the fear of losing my progress, my control, or my sought-after slim body overruled any second guessing. *Flushhhh.* I watched as the bread-paper-wad was doused in water, then swirled down the drain—my dignity spiraling closely behind.

CHAPTER 8:

HOUSEHOLD HOSTILITY

A month went by since "The Biggest Loser" and my mom was starting to get frustrated with me. My body had only changed a bit, but she was the first-hand witness to my internal transformation. I ached for her to be proud of me, my ambition, and my devotion to health. I felt like she had pressed healthy foods and exercise on me my whole life and I questioned: *Why, when I finally imitate a healthy lifestyle, do I get shamed? Wasn't **she** the one who started the program, let me join, and encouraged everyone else to lose weight!? Why wasn't I allowed to continue the things that made me a winner?*

Despite her passion for health and exercise, she saw that I was taking it too far. It had only been a month since I won the contest and I was already a completely new person. These changes sparked many arguments—Mom asking if I was after attention, telling me that I was upset because of hunger and, mostly, telling me that I needed to stop.

The arguments filled me with anger, despair, and denial. It hurt me that she would question if I lost weight for attention—I didn't *like* the attention I was getting for it! *How can she not see that!?* I adopted this new lifestyle solely for myself and my inner peace. *I didn't do anything on purpose; it was all just a result of my strong determination!* Defenses flowed out of me; she didn't understand and I, most definitely, was not *hungry*.

I would come home from school with a list of things to bring up to my mom. "Did you hear about so-and-so?" Or "I have twelve schools to apply to and three books to read and just wrote five scholarship essays." I might as well have been saying, "I know you're worried about me but don't forget about how high-achieving of a daughter I am!"

I talked about myself; bragging about my minuscule accomplishments and future plans. Most commonly, though, I dissected the flaws of my friends, my classmates, and even my own sisters in attempts to make myself seem better. I wanted to be the best, especially through the eyes of my mom. When we were together, I filled every molecule of air with some irrelevant topic, in fear that the conversation might find its way back to my health. Guarding my vulnerability and ignoring reality, I rarely left time for her to speak.

CHAPTER 9:

17 CANDLES OF CATASTROPHE

The night of my seventeenth birthday, my mom made homemade mac and cheese; the meal that was the epitome of my childhood. I don't remember a birthday where the cheesy, gooey mixture wasn't my dinner of choice. My sisters had never been huge fans, so it turned into an annual tradition that they dealt with for me. Mom's homemade mac and cheese was exclusively mine and it never failed to fill me with the warmth, comfort, and joy of motherly love.

In all my birthdays prior, I'd pile mountains of the golden cheesiness onto my plate and devour every elbow, but this year was different. I was irritated that she chose to make *that* dish for my birthday. I felt like my mom's sole purpose in doing it was to fatten me up. *She knows I don't eat pasta or cheese any more.* I believed that she cooked the meal in spite of me.

Nevertheless, I didn't want to start another argument, especially not at my birthday dinner, so I kept my mouth shut. I lifted each bite to my mouth as if the food was toxic. I collected no pleasure from the meal because all I could focus on was the fat in the clumpy cheese and the carbs in the slimy noodles. I shoveled the food into my mouth, tasting only the flavors of savory, homemade guilt.

The table conversation had drifted to the "Biggest Loser" contest again. They were talking about the contestants; who lost how much, who had already dropped out, and who had no luck. After I interrupted and asked them to shut up, Mille, my little sister, made some rude comment about me losing ten pounds.

As I ate this meal I despised and listened to my family talk about this contest I'd grown ashamed of winning, resentment began to boil in me. *It's **my** birthday and **this** is not how I want to spend it.*

Finally, I exploded, "can we please talk about something else?!" I choked down tears just as I did the macaroni. The rest of the meal was virtually silent.

I now see how demented and irrational my thoughts about my mom's motives were. My mom made the macaroni and cheese because she wanted, so badly, to still be able to restore her daughter's happiness through her favorite, homemade, comfort food. The night of my seventeenth birthday, I shattered the tiny sliver of faith that my mother still had in my sanity.

CHAPTER 10:

SPRING SHOWERS OF SHAME

Winter turned to spring and my weight, confidence, and dignity started to melt away with the snow. The abundance of clothing that I previously bought (in my aspiring-to-fit-in days) were beginning to get baggy. I sold them to a consignment shop the first minute I could. *I don't need those, anyway. I won't ever gain that weight back again.*

I didn't want people to see the extra space in my jeans and mostly, I didn't want to see the evidence of all the weight I'd lost. I tried persuading myself to accept and embrace my new body, but it didn't seem real. It didn't seem like *me*. I'd walk past myself in a mirror or in the reflection of a glass door and have to do a double-take, unsure who the skeleton staring back at me was.

By this point, I was well aware that I needed to up my intake. I started eating lunch, taking a big, caloric leap with salads and homemade dressings— I was repelled by the amount of sodium in any store-bought kind.

My self-worth was now wrapped firmly around my perseverance and achievement of "health." It seemed nearly impossible to deviate from my purified routines. I was imprisoned in my own mind and, despite the fact that I knew runnings 5Ks and drinking water for lunch wasn't what I "should" have been doing, I felt secure and composed when I stuck to my self-imposed ordinance.

I did research about the food industry and eventually became obsessed with "real" food. I began to believe that all processed food was grown in Satan's garden. I saw through all marketing; I learned that the words "diet" and "low-calorie" were part of the bullshit that the food industry preached to make money off naive, self-conscious people.

I felt like a genius because I'd figured out that real food was *the* answer to a healthy, happy life. I was an addict; roasted vegetables my drug of choice, and counterfeit, pre-packaged foods my sinister sobriety. I dreamed of growing up and only buying groceries from the local farmer's market and the nearest Whole Foods. It was no longer just "calories" that were bad, I saw microscopic blemishes in almost everything and refused them.

I made my own dinner before going anywhere at night, in fear that acceptable options wouldn't be available. Social activities, for the first time, began to present me with fears...

What if the only salad dressing they have is Ranch?
What if they comment on how skinny I am?
*What if she uses **Canola Oil** to cook the chicken?!*

Any normality or neutrality I had towards food was destroyed. I spent hours in the kitchen, taunting myself by making a pan of brownies to give away, just to assure my willpower and control were still in tact. When I didn't take a lick off the spoon or a crumb off the platter, I was complaint to my inner-self and received an imaginary high-five. Unlike all the years of my childhood, I could bake the dessert without eating a single chocolatey square and that was a profound victory.

My self-authority grew sterner and the list of foods I allowed myself to eat got smaller. When the time came that I, inevitably, ate something that wasn't "allowed," the desperation I felt after would remind me why I didn't want to do it again. I never let myself forget that the short-lived high of indulgence didn't compare to the long-term low of shame that followed. I wrote in my iPhone notes the infamous quote "nothing tastes as good as skinny *feels*."

    I began to constantly calculate how I would later make up for the consumption of things that teetered my standards. Croutons and chocolate chips had to be negated by extra exercise or a cleaner meal to come. I didn't enjoy the foods that everyone else thought were delectable because all I could taste was their lack of quality. If the peanut butter I was eating was contaminated with salt, sugar, or hydrogenated oils, so was my every thought.

    My energy and thoughts started to be entirely consumed by food. I'd start eating lunch, only to be planning what I ate for dinner half way through the meal. I'd want to go to sleep after dinner so that I could wake up in the morning and have my smoothie. I struggled to focus on other things; I would read a page in a book and not even comprehend what I read because the voice in my head was screaming about something I ate.

I began messing up orders at work, misplacing my keys, and forgetting anything that wasn't on my to-do list. I would zone out and be distant in conversations. I assumed my brain fog was caused by sleep deprivation or simply by an overloaded schedule, but food was consuming more of me than I was of it and it was taking its toll on my life.

I started reading cooking magazines, watching The Food Network (on the treadmill), and crafting scrumptious dishes for other people. I gained a fondness for cooking and the mere sight of food began to spark pleasure in my mind. It was like my subconscious mind was so hungry that it impulsively idled towards food.

I declined most offers to dine out. If I somehow summoned the "courage" to do so, I'd look up the menu first to make sure the restaurant had something that satisfied my commands.

All spontaneity disappeared; food was no longer an excuse to be leisurely and social. It was no longer a source of energy and it was no longer an area of uncertainty in my life—food had become my safety blanket. When I sat by myself and ate my luscious meal of salmon and brussels sprouts, all other problems ceased to exist.

CHAPTER 11:

INTRAPERSONAL DEMONS

At prom, I looked skinny and glamorous, decked in a spray tan and a two-piece dress that flaunted my abs. At my dance recital, I was a graceful, twig-like ballerina just like all of the *real* dancers I'd seen in performances. I was meeting my internal expectations, my *goals*, yet I still wasn't fulfilled.

The pride I gained after winning "The Biggest Loser" was diffusing into the air. Contrary to my beliefs just months before, I didn't feel like my life had improved. I had lost my cellulite and my double chin and was gifted an intrapersonal demon in return. I didn't know how much weight I'd lost and didn't want to. I avoided the scale at all costs— the mirror above my dresser my only assessor of change. I'd speculate my body and sigh, *now I **really** need to fix myself*.

I wanted to gain muscle, I coveted my old voluptuous boobs, and I was embarrassed of my non-existent butt. *Modify, tweak, gain, lose, tone.* As I continued to lose weight, the drive I had to better myself only grew stronger, louder, and meaner.

I started weightlifting, even though it delivered me nothing compared to an exhausting run. I couldn't see the miles add up, the calories burn, or the allowance to eat articulate—but even that didn't stop me. Dance, a hobby I'd loved since I was two, became boring and passive to me. I couldn't walk to my car without wanting to *sprint* instead.

I lost my love of moving if its purpose wasn't to disperse calories from my body.

My health was beginning to deteriorate. I was dwindling from slender to bony. My digestive system and metabolism were going downhill and my immune system was close behind. My homeostasis was completely out of whack, and I was fried from the physical and mental exhaustion I put on myself.

These problems only fed my need to perfect, control, and restrict more. I assumed they were occurring because something I was consuming was *wrong*. This led me to believe that the solution would be a stricter, cleaner diet.

I would try to slide detox regimens into my diet without my parents or sisters noticing. Most of the time, that meant downing a full Camelbak of water for every hour of school. For a while, I convinced myself that wheat was the agitator of my widespread health problems. Although I didn't eat many carbohydrates before, this gave me the prime excuse not to eat any at all. I was able to restrict myself and pardon it by saying, "I'm, like, kind of allergic to wheat." I was jealous of the people that were *actually* gluten-free or *morally* vegan.

This cycle of deciding which items worsened my health continued through multiple food groups. I'd cut out dairy one week, elated that I didn't have to worry about if yogurt was *okay* or not. These processes of elimination soothed some of the overbearing decisions I had to make about food. My mom had hope that these experiments would help us find a common, sinful denominator to all of my health problems, but the truth was, none of them made me feel any better.

Dodging comments turned into a daily practice. I saw people inspect my figure as I walked down the hall and I began to avoid those whom I knew would have something to preach to me about. In my small town, word got around quickly, and the number of people who approached me with worries grew with every outing. Some tried to be gentle, "Patty you're okay, right?" or "I know what you're going through." I'd choke up; I didn't want to talk and they most definitely did *not* know what I was going through.

Others were less sensitive; "Damn, how much weight have you lost now?" or "You need to get some meat on you, girl!" I'd muster up some rebuttal and simultaneously fight tears from pouring down my face. I would suffocate in a helpless, desperate rage that even *I* couldn't quite understand. No one understood and, even if they did, I wouldn't let them fracture the tall, steel gates I built around myself.

Whether it was out of fear, politeness, or just a lack of empathy, the majority of people chose not to comment at all. Instead, my weight loss became the "elephant in the room" everywhere I went. I, undoubtedly knew that I was the talk of the book clubs, the teachers' lounges, and the gossip sessions around town. People went to my friends and sisters with concern instead of confronting me. Looks of pity, concern, and complete body speculations cut my soul the deepest. The status and identity that I once worked so hard to obtain were slipping through my bony fingers.

The ample negative attention I received kindled another devil on the side of my shoulder— one who made sure I was always, painfully aware of my too-skinny identity. The offer of a cupcake, or even just the presence of a greasy pizza in the room, provoked that devil and my suspicions of everyone judging my frail body. I was constantly paranoid that people were trying to test whether or not I really had an eating disorder. I was scared to go to the bathroom after I ate because I didn't want people to think I was bulimic. I was afraid to decline the cupcake because I didn't want people to think I was anorexic.

I developed two levels of shame. In the first level, I wanted, so badly, to soothe the riot within me and simply say "no" to the cupcake. Or maybe just take the cupcake and throw it into the nearest trashcan. Then, in the second level, sat a fear that refusal would be translated as validation for people's assumptions about me.

Comments, glances, and exchanges about my body replayed over and over in my mind. I thought of ways to prove myself to others; *if people see me eating candy, maybe they'll finally realize that I don't have an eating disorder!*

My internal equilibrium got discombobulated, to say the least. The weight loss caused my hormones to jostle around as though they were in The Fred's cocktail shakers.

I would run my fingers through my hair or rub shampoo into it, and collect strand after strand in my hands. I can still remember the nauseating feeling of outright distress when this became a recurring phenomenon. *What is wrong with me?* First went my fat, then my sanity, then my muscle, then my period, and finally...my *hair*.

The chunks of fallout grew in both size and occurrence and my thin hair became almost as troubling and embarrassing as my thin body. I found ways to style it to make it seem thicker and stuck to them. I tried eating more protein and olive oil and other things that Pinterest swore would work. Mostly, however, I tried to avoid thinking about it.

Nevertheless, I'd be walking in the mall and someone with glossy, goddess-like hair would swish past me, or I'd notice the hefty pony-tail of a six-year-old in my dance class, and insecurity would rise like acidic bile in my throat.

I wouldn't let anyone touch my hair; I hated it and I hated myself for being the creator of its ugliness. I ached for the little-girl feeling I used to get when my mom French braided my hair, or the way I thought a curling iron turned me into a California beach babe. Tangles, texture, and split-ends were added to the list of things I took for granted. Down the drain went most of my blonde locks and all of my confidence.

My malnutrition was unmistakeable but, unlike my original weight loss, I never heard comments about my hair loss. Despite its blatancy, it was the last thing anyone would ever mention to me and the last thing I would ever discuss.

Another aesthetic defect populated and didn't go away. Bruises—the embodiment of sadness, illness, and punishment—found their way to my body. As the weather got warmer and summer grew closer, they appeared on my arms, thighs, and calves. Most of the time, I struggled to think of what on earth they possibly could have been from. I'd wake up with a whole new set of bluish spots on my legs and be utterly terrified. I remember, on multiple occasions, attempting to cover them with foundation. I wished I could wear pants all the time.

Everyone was concerned why my legs looked like I had just lost a kickboxing match, especially my mother. But you could always count on me to devise an explanation and advocate that I was "perfectly fine." I'd laugh it off and say things like, "I got in a bike wreck," or "I tripped at work," or "I just bruise easily," and then change the subject. People had their suspicions, I'm sure, but my urging defenses made them get the picture; I didn't want to talk about it. My friends and family eventually learned to stop asking.

If a normal person's hair started falling out or their skin started to bruise, rushing to a doctor would be a given...but not for me. After all, the doctor was practically my enemy. I was now so sensitively vulnerable about my appearance that I wouldn't face it or it's dogmatist.

I refused to admit the principle that I, and everyone else, knew to be the cause of my thin hair, bruised legs, and overall dysfunction. Despite my smiling face, my productivity, and my 1K followers on Instagram, *I was not okay*.

I was now *too skinny*, and it was more miserable than anything I'd ever felt before. My world of desolation and humiliation ignited my need for comfort and security. Eventually, there was only one thing that could bring me that: food.

CHAPTER 12:

STICKY, SKINNY, SUMMERTIME

I was ecstatic for school to end so that I could get back in control of my life which had started to unravel. I was relieved that I no longer had to be in the spotlight of shaming eyes for eight hours a day, but bikinis and tank tops presented me with a whole new rush of new feelings.

I was secretly excited that I finally got to show off my six pack and thigh gap. I knew my bikini pictures on Instagram had the potential to make other girls jealous. I was aware of this because, for so long, *that* girl was me. *I* was the one gaping at the flawless figures and smiling faces of models, sorority sisters, and famed singers on social media. Knowing that I got to sport the thing that other girls wanted was a tiny—and overall unsatisfying—drop of water in my vast desert of self-consciousness.

I also was scared; summer meant I no longer had layers of clothes to hide my flaws under. I imagined bruises and bones sparkling in the sun for everyone to see. My body would have bystanders and I knew its raw form would spark even more worries. As if I wasn't uncomfortably aware of myself already, my thinness now had no disguise.

Despite my mom's wishes, my ill-fitting shorts, and what I knew was *right*, I didn't break most of my "healthy" habits. I continued to do an ab workout every time I saw the little, blue, three-pound weights sitting on my floor, I continued to refuse orange juice because of its sugar content, and I continued going to the 5:00 a.m. H.I.I.T. class.

One morning, the class and I were all on our jog back from the steep hill that we ran up and down at least ten times. As my fifty-something neighbor jogged passed me, she said, "School just got out, what—last week? You're suppose to be hanging out with friends and sleeping in! Why are you still doing *this* and not enjoying your summer?!"

This took me back. I choked on the humid air. *This **is** what I enjoy doing*, I thought to myself. *Right?* But she was right, I was probably the only seventeen year old who woke up at five in the morning the first week of summer break. I laughed off her comment and kept up my jog, but her words wouldn't escape my mind—they made me realize how much I really *was* maturing for my age. As I ran, the narrator within me reasoned:

I do love mornings and coffee and vegetables,
...focus Patience, only one more mile...
And I do also love baths and reading and cooking,
...don't worry Patience, you're still yourself, just healthier...
*And **I am** beginning to prefer staying in my healthy comfort zone over going out and being social...*

...yikes...

With half a mile left in the run, I had to bite my tongue to not cry. My neighbor's words were my first sign that calories weren't the only thing I was depriving myself of—maybe I was depriving myself of my youth, too. I tried to shake these scary thoughts out of my head, to focus on the home stretch of the run, but I was now sickened by the realization that my outgoing personality and adolescent spirit were beginning to diminish.

CHAPTER 13:

THE COWARDLY CAMP COUNSELOR

After a couple of weeks in my small-town sun, it was June and I was going to work at three consecutive week-long camps. This break of routine gave my desperate mom and I hope. The whole month prior, I refused doctors appointments and weigh-ins, banking on the fact that, surely, three weeks without real exercise, plus a diet composed of college cafeteria food would gain me at least ten pounds. I was exhausted from always thinking about food and was eager to focus on something else.

The first camp was a leadership workshop where I was the counselor of about twenty high school students. In one sense, it was refreshing—I felt more free of judgement there than I had at home. I met new people who assumed I was just one of those girls who had *always* been thin. A lot of people didn't know me before the week had even started, so my body didn't scream for their attention.

In another sense, I was scared of how all the people I *did* know would perceive me and my changes. I was both excited and nervous to be reunited with my old camp friends who hadn't seen me in a year—when I was more than fifteen pounds heavier.

Since I wasn't close enough to anyone at camp, no one verbally commented on my weight, but people's expressions were transparent. My body became, yet again, the awkward topic that everyone was acutely aware of but no one, especially not myself, felt comfortable bringing up.

The camp staff had free range of a "snack room" equipped with all the powdered donuts, Chex Mix, and Gatorade that any kid could ever ask for. I remember walking in on the first night, starving after a busy day of morale-increasing and leadership-building activities. I remember feeling dumbstruck at the sight of all the food; my mouth watered even though most of them were processed, forbidden foods.

My first instinct, or maybe it was my second, was that *none* of it was acceptable. It didn't even strike me that I had options. I tried to convince myself out of the anxiety that was lurking; *you're going to bed soon, do you really need to eat anyway?* But my hunger was roaring. My eyes darted around the room until they finally landed on a big can of Planter's peanuts. *These will do.* I tore open the package and grabbed a handful.

I returned to the snack corner every single night and, by the end of the week, the big blue can was empty.

One day, I was in a meeting with my whole group of kids, when the pretty, bubbly blonde girl in the group blurted out, "I was looking through your Instagram, and you used to be really chubby...Did something happen? Now you're like super freakin' skinny." Everyone hushed. My cheeks flushed and I struggled to laugh it off. The girl tried to play it off by saying, "but you look so much better now!" but that only stung worse. I was supposed to be the fearless leader, the role model that these kids looked up to, but in that moment, I felt them all sensing my foolish anguish.

In return, the group tried to make *her* ashamed of her curiosity. I made sure she knew I didn't care that she'd asked; it was, after all, the truth. I replied with the same excuse that I'd spit out a thousand times: "Yeah, I was never *meaning* to lose weight, but this past year I really started to exercise more and eat healthier and it just kinda happened...Blah blah blah."

65

Later, when I was alone on my walk to my dorm, I choked out the cry that I'd been biting back since the moment Blonde Bubbles proposed her question. *Was I really* **chubby** *back then?* I wondered. I knew I was a little soft around the edges, but even *then* I don't think I ever considered myself "chubby."

I was feeling pathetic and wanted sympathy from someone—anyone—but I couldn't get it; no one would understand how I felt. *I* couldn't even find the words to sum up my feelings. My scrawny, defective body was called to the whole group's attention and even stronger than the feelings of humiliation, were those of total isolation. At this camp with the nicest, most accepting people surrounding me, I somehow felt alone.

I wanted to call my mom; I wanted to call my best friend, Emma. I wanted to talk to anyone at the camp but I was too afraid to because I knew that their responses would all be the same: I needed to gain some weight.

The camps proceeded and my mind was still drowning in a wave pool of worry; I was past the point of resuscitation. For the sake of seeming "normal," I physically allowed myself to eat the popsicles and popcorn that everyone else was, but emotionally they tore me apart.

The last camp I went to, I counseled a group of fourth grade girls. I went to this same camp when I was younger and it had never failed to be my favorite part of the summer. During the dance breaks, which we called "Energizers," I would mentally formulate how much of a work-out the silly moves were giving me. The careless, child-like amusement of Energizers, and the whole camp in general, was muddled in my obsession.

Almost every morning, I told myself that I would wake up and run the campus before the busy day started. I reminded myself how much better my day would be if it started with some exercise. Regardless of these preposterous thoughts, in the span of this camp (and the two camps before), I never once went on a run.

I couldn't admit the truth—the truth that I never got myself out of bed because I really, really did not want to get up early and go *run* during summer camp. The fact that I was at camp helped me reason with my harsh inner-critic: *It's okay!*

You're on a break from responsibility! I tried to remind myself that I could relax, but whispers of shame always came back when I swayed from my own authority. I'd sneak into my dorm room to do some burpees, planks, or jumping jacks on the hard tile of the dormitory and they would, momentarily, calm me.

CHAPTER 14:

HOME SWEET REALITY

I arrived home from camp eager to tell my mom about the adventures I'd had. I was excited to have three weeks full of things that we could discuss to distract from the conversation of my body. But when I walked through the door on that muggy, July day, her expression squashed all hope. She nudged her glasses down the bridge of her nose and examined my body. "You don't look like you've gained any weight, Patience," she said sternly.

I was flustered. *Nice to see you too, Mom!* My weight was *not* what I wanted to talk about first thing through the door. Regardless, I assured her "There is really no way I didn't! I ate hot dogs and popsicles with the kids and didn't even go on a run once!" I wanted to defend myself by recollecting every single grain of rice and peanut M&M that I surmounted at camp. I wanted her to be proud of me.

That same day, after my failed objections, we went to her office at The Y so that she could weigh me. I gained the panicky feelings that eventually became the conditioned response to seeing a scale. I begged my mom to not make me do it. I assured her that I had gained weight and—if not—postpone the weighing a week and I guaranteed I would.

Finally, I gave up—after all, I was fairly certain that I'd picked up a few pounds. I took off my shoes and lifted my feet, one at a time, onto the hard plastic of the scale. With a lump in the back of my throat, I watched the numbers go up and up.

Think heavy. Then, the numbers in the digital window stopped changing and the lump in my throat disappeared, leaving me completely breathless.

The screen read 108 LBS. My seventeen-year-old, five foot ten body had lost thirty pounds since January. Thirty pounds that I didn't—ever—have to lose. *There's no way*. I looked to my mom. Her eyes were no longer filled with looks of shame and frustration but were now glassy, blue ponds of woe.

For the first time, I was actually scared. I hadn't weighed 108 pounds since probably the seventh grade. *What have I done to myself?*

My mom's shaken face justified that the nerves I'd felt before were, indeed, rational. Although she had clearly seen the lack of normality in me, she was now utterly terrified for the same reason I was; *how could I come home from camp and actually weigh **less** than I did before?!*

The anger around the situation shifted into fear and the fact that something may have been seriously wrong. She scheduled a doctor's appointment for the very next day.

The thought of going to see a doctor made my stomach lurch. In one respect, I almost felt relief; going to the doctor meant that there was hope—that all my health problems might have been derived from something other than my eating habits. I remember thinking to myself, *maybe I have some infection, or a parasite, or a biological mishap that is causing me to lose weight,* and actually, sickeningly wanting this to be true.

I wanted to have a legitimate excuse for my weighing 108 pounds. A medical condition at least had the potential to grant me people's sympathy, but an eating disorder? *Not so much*. I didn't want to have to change the way I ate; it was what I loved.

I did everything I could to not go to the doctor's that day. "Give me a Philly cheesesteak, a Frito-chili-pie—anything! I'll eat it, right now!" I pleaded, and if that's what it would have taken, then I really would have. But it was too late; my mom was done trusting my pleas.

Despite my resistance, the next day I found myself, hands shaking, in the waiting room of my doctor with my mom. I was somewhere between infuriated and terrified about being there. The nurse called my name and I felt dizzy as I stood up and walked to get weighed and measured.

I prayed that when I stepped on the doctor's scale, the number would magically be larger than it had in my mom's office. *Maybe Mom's scale is broken*, I fooled myself. All optimism for the day was shattered, though, when I looked down at my feet—the nurse's scale read 106 pounds.

I swallowed the achy feeling of emerging tears as I walked in the office. My mom and I spoke to the doctor about my situation. Yes, I ran cross country. Yes, I exercised a lot. Yes, I ate mostly healthy food. No, I didn't skip meals (anymore). No, I didn't think I was fat, and, worst of all... No, I wasn't having a period anymore.

The smell of Lysol and latex suffocated me and the lump in my throat grew so large that I let my mom do most of the talking, in fear that I might cry. Regardless, I still had to throw in my disclaimers. I tried to express to him how, *yes*, I was aware that my behavior back in the winter was a little overboard, but I wasn't like that now. *I'm practically scared to skip a meal now!*

"You can have all the Oreos, milkshakes, and cheeseburgers your heart desires," the balding physician said with a chuckle. *Easier said than done*. I was annoyed at his lack of empathy.

"But that's just the thing. Those *aren't* what I crave. It's not like I prefer whole foods because I think they'll help me get skinnier—they're what I *actually* enjoy!" I replied.

He acted like he understood, but I was weary. It felt like he was speaking to me in the same tone that he would a little kid. I perceived him saying something like, "Ma'am, your daughter is anorexic, but don't worry—it's just a phase and a common one for young girls," to my mother if I left the room. *I'm not stupid!* I wanted to scream in his face. I tried to express to him how I just wanted to be *normal* again; how I didn't want to stuff myself, starve myself, or be constantly thinking about food.

After the storytelling ended, I was afraid of what his opinion of me would be. He first assured us that it was common for female runners to lose their periods. This made me feel a tiny bit better, until he reinforced the bottom line; 106 pounds was extremely dangerous for my height. Regardless of what I *preferred* to eat, I needed to increase my intake and start gaining weight.

"I understand," I muttered as I fiddled with the paper on the examination table. Lastly, he said, "Since you don't think you need to lose weight, I don't *think* you have an eating disorder," I was elated. I knew my mom heard him say that and I wanted to nudge her and say *told you so*! "—but, if you can't get yourself to put on some weight, for the sake of your health, my conclusion will likely change."

A broad spectrum of emotions washed over me. It was a smack in the face; I couldn't keep dancing around the actual work of putting on weight. I reminded myself that if I could rearrange my mind to love things I once hated, *surely* I could switch it around again.

The three of us discussed some measures that I could take to accomplish this. I told him that, for me, it was easier to give up a workout than it was to eat a plate of Fettuccine Alfredo. He wrote something on his clipboard and nodded. He then said that he wanted me to quit exercising everyday, document my intake, and come in for a weigh-in at least once a week.

This bothered me. *Weren't appointments and diaries going to cause me to place **more** attention on food?!* But I didn't argue as I knew that, at this point, I had no other option.

I walked out of his office slightly disappointed; I didn't have a medical excuse or a cure-all pill. I was the only one who could clean up this horrible mess I'd made.

After that day at the doctor's, I gained a shadow that was always following me and reminding me that my weight had better not drop one milligram. For the next couple of weeks, I was morally torn; I *did* want to dwindle back into food normality, but also felt like I should have been consuming unorthodox portions because I needed to gain weight...*fast*.

I remember one day, sitting in my house feeling bored, passive, and confined to the walls around me. Knowing I wasn't allowed to work-out made me fancy the thought of sneaking out to go run or doing an At-Home Ab Sculptor.

I tried to distract myself by cleaning my room and making art, but the desire to exercise was pounding in the back of my head. Finally, I gave up and was submissive to my corrupt thoughts. I ran up and down our staircase, skipping every other step on the way.

I counted each time I bounded up the flight, telling myself, *just five more*, after each. I kept going and going until eventually, I was too out of breath to continue. I was gasping for air and drenched in sweat from the humidity of our house.

I was spending my summer running stairs instead of going to the pool, fishing, or gravel-roading with cute boys, and I didn't care. I didn't care because the stairs brought me the only thing I yearned for; the stairs brought me closure in my newly established world of unease.

CHAPTER 15:

A BODY AS EVIDENCE

Anxiety sprouted deep in my brain and quickly grew into a relentless weed that I couldn't unroot. I felt like every move I made was wrong. "Healthy" foods were not allowed, according to my doctor, Mom, and everyone else, but "unhealthy" foods were not condoned by the little voice in my head and its delicate boundaries of guilt. I stopped going to the H.I.I.T. class and stopped doing cardio in the public eye altogether.

The nagging, begging, voice in my head simply could not be quieted. One day, I was going on a "meditative walk" on the trail behind my house. In reality, that was just the excuse I'd presented to my mom so that I could get *some* kind of exercise in my day. I walked, took deep breaths, and tried to take in my surroundings, but all I could think about was how much I wanted to run. Every fiber in my body craved to pick up the pace, to feel the calories burn, to feel like something was getting done. It felt like my mind and body were completely disconnected—my body, begging me to run, and my mind reminding me that I wasn't suppose to.

Having to make the decision of whether or not I would run, once again, dug up queasy feelings of uncertainty. *What if my mom catches me running? What if the neighbors see? Then they'll know for sure I have a problem.*

Then... I did it; my leisurely walk evolved into an intentional jog. It felt like I had control again—like my time was now being spent to its full capacity. I picked up my pace and soon my feet were sprinting over the rocks and dirt of the trail. I felt productive. I wasn't doing piddly, half-hearted fitness; I was dominating calories, miles, time— *measurable* things that I had power over. After about two miles, when I knew no one would see, I stopped and did some squats and lunges. On the compact dirt of my backyard trail, I was being rebellious to the outside world but obedient to myself. It felt right.

I started eating more. I still refused chicken nuggets and crab rangoons, of course, but I began consuming more—a lot more—of the things I was already eating before. If I was going to gain weight, I would do it *my* way. I stared at the Oreos in the shelf at the grocery store. *Did the doc realize that half of the ingredients in this shit are carcinogens?* I planned to do it healthily, which commonly resulted in an entire jar of organic almond butter, two whole sweet potatoes, or a bag of sugar snap peas devoured in one sitting.

Physically, I was more flexible about what I digested. After all, I knew people would *definitely* assume I had an eating disorder if they still saw me declining stuff. Emotionally, though, nothing changed. I was still sickened with fear when Dad handed me the biscuits during our Sunday morning family breakfast. When I ate these "unacceptable" foods, everything in me yelled, *spit it out! What are you doing!?* But my voluntary muscles yielded to my audience's opinions.

My mom raised me to be independent; I paid for my own things, did my own work, maintained good grades, and she didn't need to check in on me. That was just how it was, and that was just how we both liked it. Because of our relationship, I knew she desperately wanted to trust me when I promised I'd gain weight.

She didn't want to have to start telling me what she expected from me. She didn't want to admit that her daughter, her "baby girl #2," might actually have an eating disorder. Never would she have tried to manage what I ate, unless it was the only option left. My mom wanted, as much as I did, to believe that I could solve this problem on my own.

We never went back to that doctor.

Mom and I were now consistently arguing about my intake. She would ask me what I ate for lunch and, because I didn't want to admit that I had grilled chicken and sautéed asparagus again, I would act violated by her question. "Don't you trust me?"

Despite my claims, she needed evidence of this progress I bellowed about. I'd walk to her office, hoping that my mom hadn't yet summoned the initiative to make me step on the scale, but every so often, she caught me. When this happened,

I would pray to God that I'd at least put on a pound or two.

I never went below the infamous 106 pounds, but I was probably gaining milligrams per day. I climbed on the scale one day, weighed 112, and bragged to my mom; "See! I *am* eating more! Any progress is good progress!" Then, this optimism died the next week as I looked down at a whopping 110 lbs.

This routine of disappointment continued, and my mom's frustration increased. I knew fear churned in her stomach and concern fluttered through her sun-spotted chest when she saw the numbers. I knew my mom hated weighing me just as much as I did.

CHAPTER 16:

SENIOR YEAR

Summer was nearing its end and senior year was about to begin. I was skinnier than ever, and my confidence in my body had reached an all time low. I was going in as Student Body President—a role model to the entire school. I also started cross country, excited to finally have an excuse to work out. Running seemed to pardon my thinness.

One time, I was serving two old women at The Fred and, after I took their orders, one of them just looked at me and said, "How are you so skinny, girl?" This was one of numerous customers who commented on how adorable I was, how I should model, or how they wouldn't be asking *me* how the truffle fries taste. My hollow cheeks flushed. I laughed it off and replied that I ran cross country. They exchanged phrases of "Ohhhh!" and "Of course," like the sport gave my malnourished body all the sense in the world. I began to cling to the saying "I run" like it was my personal motto.

After the long hot runs at cross county practice, my friend Zac and I would weight lift in the school's gym. This became another ritual that I felt like I *should* do; *I better weight lift because all this running will disintegrate my muscle!*

As we went about our circuits, I'd blab the whole time about college plans or how annoying it was that everyone thought I had an eating disorder, and Zac always listened. When we weren't gossiping, he taught me the proper techniques to weight lifting. At first, I acted interested, but towards the end of the season, I'd roll my eyes, say "I don't care if my form is correct," and continue to talk about myself.

Eventually, Zac became the only person I would talk to about my body and food. I cherished the time we talked because he never judged me. He never made fun of the fact that I could barely lift the bar and he never disregarded me as the melodramatic teenage girl I was.

When I talked about food, Zac was genuinely concerned, as I was when he spoke of his battles. At 4:30 p.m. in the high school weight room, I felt like I could *actually* be myself. He made me feel okay, like I wasn't some freak who weighed a hundred pounds and, most favorably, he believed me every single time I told him I was working hard to gain weight.

After a while, I began to dread the actual chore of weight lifting. I hated spending my time enlarging my imaginary muscles and I hated not being able to lift as much as I thought I should. Sure, I wanted to transform into the girl whose biceps bust out of her long-sleeved shirts, but I couldn't get past the lack of pleasure I had in the task.

Despite how much I valued that time for Zac and I's conversations, I began to secretly hope, everyday, that he would have to bail. I secretly hoped that the football team would be working out or that Mille would call me needing a ride home. I secretly hoped that I could admit how much I despised lifting weights.

CHAPTER 17:

THE TOTAL PACKAGE

I was seemingly thriving in every aspect of my life and, most of the time, I believed that my lifelong pursuit of perfection was finally unfolding. I was Student Body President and had gained a grasp of my mission in school—no longer did I care to party every weekend or impress my peers. It was now time to prepare for college, time to get serious.

Academics paralleled my newfound self-discipline. Calculus and chemistry came as no struggle to me because my mindset had completely altered since the start of the prior school year. Meeting my social, personal, and educational goals seemed of no difficulty anymore. *If I could lose ten pounds in a month, surely, I can do this*, I told myself.

In the time I wasn't thinking about food, I was doing things that I thought would benefit my future. I worked diligently in school because I didn't want to be just *pretty* anymore, I wanted to be "the smart one" too. I wanted to be valued for my intelligence in *addition* to my looks. "The total package" was my dream superlative, and at this point, I knew if I wanted something, I could get it with the magic power of hard work.

I was an avid to-do list maker and made plans months ahead. Studying for the ACT, writing papers two weeks in advance, and figuring out college plans were items to cross off my list. I read book after book, getting more satisfaction from the placement of my bookmark in the stack of pages than the actual content of the story. I was far too busy hustling to pause for the sake of a good movie, a deep breath, or to simply appreciate my surroundings. I gained a new emblem of self-worth: productivity.

I lost the leisure in my undying love of creating artwork. Every project was made to sell, to give as a gift, or to serve a functional purpose. I'd text my mom pictures of a new thing I made at least once a week and she'd reply, "you're a machine!" My deeply-rooted passion for art was getting diluted like pigment in water.

I saw everything as something to complete and most parts of my social, emotional, and physical life paid for it. Regardless, there's no denying that the rigorous discipline I emplaced in myself sparked some change for the better. I started excelling more in school than I ever had before, all because I *told* myself that I was smart. I was constantly reminding myself that I could do anything and had, not dreams, but *plans* of going to school far away and becoming a naturopathic doctor.

I instilled my own unique manner of "cool" because I was now a senior and there was no one I cared enough to conform my morals to. My social and aesthetic aspirations were already accomplished and I was now renovating myself to be exactly how I wished on the inside. Like the quote "you're your own worst critic," I was my *only* critic and put more pressure on myself than anyone else ever had.

I became so wrapped up in myself that I was no longer concerned about who I hung out with or who cared. I tried to talk to everyone at school and to form as many relationships as possible. My worst fear was that people thought I was conceited, so I made sure to be at every social event and tried to cure any negative impressions people had of me. My own vanity—because I wanted to be seen as *nice*—was the thing that inspired my vast outreach in high school. Somehow, this all led me to win Homecoming Queen.

I had the ideal body (according to magazines, social media, and other photo-shopped outlets), I was one of the smartest people in my grade, I had good friends, and I had—finally—gained the small town glory that I once lusted for. From an outside perspective, I had it all, and I was dying to convince myself of the same. I wanted nothing more than to feel as wonderful as others perceived me to be, but something was always, ever-so-slightly, off.

Since I led the Pledge of Allegiance on the first day of school, the looks of my teachers and my peers proved that I could not lie about my body's condition any longer. My thin hair, bruised legs, and tiny figure stirred more concern and everything that I was eager to ditch at the end of my junior year returned and intensified. Despite my attempts to gain weight at the end of the summer, only a few pounds had actually stuck.

I had an abundance of baggy clothes, worrisome looks, and insecurities, but I wouldn't dare let anyone know. My weight loss was now simultaneously the essence of who I was and the one thing I hated to talk or think about.

I adopted the unrealistic mindset that every single decision I made was going to make or break me as a person. Like I wasn't going to be able to pay for college if I spent more than ten dollars on anything, or like eating a pinch too little or a teaspoon too much would wreck my body. The presence of food made me nervous if I had just eaten an hour before, all the same as it would if it was supposed to be lunch, dinner, or breakfast time and I had nothing around. Anxiety began to regularly pinch me as yet another technique of self-sabotage.

CHAPTER 18:

PANIC IN THE WEIGHT ROOM

One day, Sammy (my older sister) and I were working out; I was doing crunches while she passed me a ten-pound medicine ball. She'd throw the ball at me, I'd lay back, crunch, then throw it back. *Catch, crunch, throw, catch, crunch, throw, catch, crunch, throw.* As we continued the monotonous exercise, strange feelings started to boil somewhere deep within me. Little bubbles of panic started to burst in my body. I couldn't fully grasp the pain; it just felt like something bad was going to happen if I kept crunching. Regardless, I kept doing it and the pangs of panic multiplied. *What's going on?* I wanted to know. Catch, crunch, throw, panic. *WHAT IS GOING ON!?*

I was scared because I didn't know why I was scared. In this state of oblivion, I remember thinking: *I'm having a panic attack*, then, five seconds later, chastising myself for even having such ludicrous thoughts.

I had an absurd judgement of anxiety (*me, Patience Dorman, having a physiological disorder? Ha!*) but feelings of uneasiness, of an inexplicable doom, continued. Fear throbbed in my head as the blood through my veins: fast and hard.

Finally, my body locked up and I felt like I had no other choice so I told my sister to stop. "I'm just done with this exercise," I stuttered out.

To explain how anxiety feels is sort of like explaining how water tastes. Nevertheless, my relationship with anxiety could be described as an anticipated sense of unease and instability—like a swarm of buzzing bees that I clearly saw in front of me but was still forced to walk through. In the first semester of my senior year, this sensation started to become reoccurring.

I would stand up after sitting in my desk for an hour and get those jitters accompanied by a fog of dizziness. After this happened a couple of times, I started to fear standing up from my seat because I knew those unsettling feelings would return. I recognized that this was all in my mind, but I still couldn't get away from it. This made me both extremely frustrated and frightened, as my underlying thought was that I was too smart to have some taboo diagnosis of "anxiety."

No matter how much I scolded myself and reminded myself that I was just being delusional, the anxiety, and the fear of anxiety, wouldn't go away. I'd end a workout feeling paranoid that something was wrong: *I didn't do enough reps on bench press*, or *I shouldn't be working out at all*, or *I hope no one saw me do that cool down run*.

Another common one was, *I need protein in the next 15 minutes or else I won't gain muscle and then, what was even the point of working out?!* It was like a constant bickering streaming through my mind.

Because of this uncertainty, this *anxiety* that I'd developed, I tried to fix everything in my life. I was on a quest for stability. I would spend hours studying, ensuring my good grades. I'd spend my day researching; ensuring my worth and intellect. I'd spend the night preparing my lunch for the next day; ensuring I had the exact nutrients I believed my body needed.

In times that I felt my sense of control sliding from my grip, I had habits that I ran to. The way kids chew their fingernails, I instilled rituals of reassurance that helped me cope with the uncertainty that my reality had become…

I would touch my stomach and the feeling of my hard abs under my shirt would immediately relieve me. I would update my Profile Picture and be reminded that people still liked me via hundreds of virtual "likes." I would lift my shirt up in the mirror and examine my flat, toned tummy. I would read an article about how I wasn't going to get cancer or diseases because I ate *real* food. I would flex my little arm muscles and feel the distinct line between my bicep and tricep. I would feel better. I latched onto these private ceremonies of comfort desperately.

The elements of my life were now all on track; my intellect, grades, and hopes for the future at an all-time high. My external face was happy, bubbly, and flourishing, and I was the best acquaintance to everyone (hence Homecoming Queen and Student Body President). Most of the time, I really had myself convinced that this was how my life was going to be. Then, something would happen, and I'd remember how scary of a thought that actually was.

One day, after a long swim in the lap pool, a realization popped into my head; *if I want to be a well-respected woman with a great body when I* *grow up, this can't just be a **phase**.* The thought sent shivers down my back.

I thought that if I wanted to have any kind of muscle, I was going to have to lift weights for the rest of my life. I thought that if I was going to avoid obesity, I was going to have to decline cheesecake for the rest of my life. It seemed unfathomable to instill this self-discipline for the rest of my life, but at the same time, it seemed like my only choice.

I tried to picture myself in college loading up a plate at the salad bar and working out in the recreation center. I tried to picture myself going to the movies and snacking on a bag of trail mix as my date eats popcorn alone. I tried to picture myself as a mom, making birthday cakes out of all-natural protein powder and taking yoga classes. I didn't want to admit it, but my future seemed both un-accomplishable and miserable.

CHAPTER 19:

REPLACED

My physical and mental health had dipped lower than the percentage of fat on my body—dangerously low. My closest relationships, those deeper than face-value, were beginning to suffer, and the pulse of compassion between my family and I, or my best friend and I, was withering...

One weekend, my sisters, mom, and dad were all going to Kansas City to visit our cousins, but I had to stay home to take the ACT on Saturday. I was annoyed at the timing of their trip but I also had been preparing months for this test, so there was no way I'd miss it. My best friend, Emma (who has always been close with my family), ended up tagging along so that she could get a homecoming dress in the City. I had shrugged off the jealousy I felt when they first proposed the idea to me. I pictured Emma sitting in *my* spot between my sisters at dinner. *Then again*, I refocused my attention, *I need to focus on this test and, honestly, do I really want to order **another** sandwich to spite my family?*

The weekend went by, mine revolving solely around my all-determining standardized test on Saturday morning. When my family and Emma came home on Sunday night, they didn't shy away from expressing just how fun the trip, without me, was. I bit back the irrational envy I felt creeping through me when Emma told me how fun going out to eat and shopping was with *my* family.

"I just feel like you're so different than Sammy and Mille. Like, I did stuff with them that I feel like you would have *neverrrr* done," Emma said.

Her words were a stab in the heart. "What's that supposed to mean?"

But in all honesty, the phrase had punctured me so deeply because I knew, without any explanation, *exactly* what it meant. I knew what she was referring to, and I didn't want to admit that it was the truth. Emma was reminiscing on the fact that they all went out to eat and didn't have to talk or think about health.

She was talking about how she felt completely comfortable and un-judged ordering a bacon cheeseburger at the restaurant. She was talking about how she could blow her money on clothes and didn't receive snide remarks about how expensive it all was. She was talking about how she could still be a kid around them.

I knew that over the weekend, Emma had witnessed my sisters spraying whipped cream in each other's mouths and balancing the creamy towers over fits of laughter. I grew angry and infinitely defensive because I knew that Emma felt like I would never do those things anymore. *I would've been fun too! I'm just like them! Did you forget that I'll eat things besides just salad now?!*

I was offended and I made sure she knew it. I objected to everything, but we both knew that her words rang the absolute truth; I wasn't invested in the naive, the childish, and especially not the caloric parts of our friendship any longer.

CHAPTER 20:

AN ODE TO GOOD FRIENDS

Although my input into relationships fluctuated, my best friends retained their genuine love for me no matter the condition of my body. My friends never commented on how I looked, likely because I dodged the topic like the foam balls in our annual StuCo Dodgeball Tournament. It became a known fact among us that I liked to eat healthy. They were appalled by my willpower and were, more than likely, worried about me. Regardless, they trusted my word—or maybe were just courteous of my feelings—and didn't gawk.

They acted interested in the different types of homemade salad dressing I brought to lunch and they poked fun at the fact that I had dibs on their left over vegetables. If they thought I had an eating disorder, I would have never known. They accepted and respected the fact that I ate healthy and that I didn't want to talk about it.

At the time, I underestimated the gift that my friends were in my life. I've heard stories about girls who lose weight and other girls in school bully them, call them anorexic, and shun them.

Because of this, I believe my whole experience would have been considerably different —considerably *worse*—had I not had such good friends by my side. They didn't let my appearance impact our relationships and for that, I'm so grateful.

CHAPTER 21:

BELIEF SYSTEM (OR LACK THEREOF)

Out of all the elements of my life, the most prevalent suffering, undeniably, occurred in my spirituality. I grew up going to church every Sunday, but as we got older, our schedules got busier, the priest of our childhood left, and church became excruciatingly boring. My family became a Chreaster family—people that only go to church on Christmas and Easter.[1]

I was fine with this and I didn't try to claim any identity of being super religious. In fact, I was growing accustomed to worship the ideas of knowledge, achievement, and productivity instead. Although I would have never openly admitted it, I didn't really know if Christianity fell into those categories.

As a child, I payed more attention to my drawing on the offering envelopes than I did to the sermon. I didn't really understand the word of the Bible and began to doubt the miraculousness of the bit that I did. I had a second-hand, mediocre, belief in God and my abundance of other problems were much more worthy of my attention.

---

[1] I did not make this phrase up. I'm not that funny. Don't give me credit.

I remember the first time I'd ever heard something outside of the religious norms of my small town...

I was at a statewide, weekend-long Student Council event and was rooming with a good friend of mine, Haley Watson. Haley is one of the most inspiring young people I've ever gotten the chance to meet. She is the kind of person who, when she's speaking on something she's interested in, you can feel the passion oozing out of her. She has so much life and depth behind every word that comes out of her mouth; you can't help but be in awe when she talks. During one of her blabs, she began talking about religion, a subject that I was well aware of my ignorance on.

I assumed what she said next was from her logical intuition. (Yes, my 17 year old, brainiac self was dissociating religion from intellect).

"You know, I've always kind of had my doubts about God and Heaven and everything, but I'm really starting to understand how good it feels just to believe in *something*," Haley said.

I'm sure Haley didn't think much of what she said and I know she would've never imagined that her words would have impacted me as much as they did. It was the first part of her statement that resonated with me. The fact that Haley—the super smart, super pretty, super involved Haley Watson— confessed that she didn't always feel strong in her beliefs about God. *Woah.* Feelings of relief rushed over me because my friend's vulnerability and openness validated that I was not alone in my hesitancy.

It was like the first half of her statement rang so loudly in my ears that I barely heard the second part. *Something about it feeling good?* It was so mind boggling because it was the first time that I'd heard someone my age, whom I respected and admired, say they doubted Jesus and The Resurrection and Heaven and all of the other frills that tag along with Christianity.

I too, had my doubts because I was used to seeing Christianity as something that people sported like a new pair of leather boots. Like "Faith" was some permission slip that exempted them from their wrong doings and lack of intellect. My thesis that, "*you* create your life with every decision *you* make,"made it difficult to comprehend the idea of a higher power. It was refreshing to hear someone else admit this, too.

Regardless of my skepticism in Christ, I thought that religion was an unwritten requirement of my small town, so I kept my mouth shut and swallowed my apprehension. I had dreams of moving to a big city, of becoming a sophisticated, successful, student, and of "finding myself" even more that I "already had." I told myself, *maybe then—when I'm smarter—then I'll have time to research religion. Then I'll have time to figure out what I **actually** believe.* At seventeen, I didn't deem "exploring my spirituality" worthy of my precious time or social status.

I began to see God, church, and all the mumbo-jumbo as an undeclared social rule. It was, yet another thing I *should* do. I prayed to God to help me pass a test or find my wallet—selfish, momentary desires. "Being a Christian" got added to my list:

- Pray every night, *check*.

- Be a leader in Fellowship of Christian Athletes, *check*.

- Go to church when I can, *check*.

I was well aware of my lack of confidence in the existence of God. As much as I wanted to feel what my preacher was saying in the gut of my stomach, I just didn't. It seemed as though I couldn't, no matter how hard I tried, foster any real beliefs, so I wasn't going to pretend that I could.

I wasn't going to put on a face that I was a church-camping going, Young-Life comrade, or use-bible-verses-in-captions kind of person. The stigma I had around "being religious," and the fear I had of being an imposter—of being a phony Christian—blocked any opportunity for Faith to sprout.

Well, that, and, the fact that my life was now being devoured by hiding, eating, choosing, minimizing, and thinking about one thing; I had no room for God because *food* had become my only salvation.

CHAPTER 22:

PRETEND PERMISSION

I now regularly ate three, and sometimes even —*I know, crazy*—four meals a day. My relationship with food had transformed, yet again, and I was now ravenous for food—food I deemed healthy, that is. It was just like when the delivery boy rang the doorbell during childhood sleepovers, or when I devoured my post-workout smoothies the winter before; the times I got to eat were the highlights of my day.

As a senior, I would come home from school with an excitement because it was time to eat my snack. I'd spend ten minutes deciding what to eat only to end up bloated from a whole bag of all-natural sweet potato chips, half a bag of grapes, and an orange in my stomach. Despite the fact that they met my "real food" criteria, I felt the same shame after inhaling copious amounts of fruits, veggies, and nuts as I did when I finished off tubs of ice cream years before.

I would be mad at myself because I'd ruined my hunger for the night, but I still couldn't resist making myself dinner. It was just like a binge of fifteen-year-old, pre-controlling Patience, but this time, I was stuffing myself full of non-GMO, gluten-free, and organic desperation instead.

My days of skipping meals now seemed unreal. I never forgot to pack my lunch the night before school, never forgot to set chicken out to defrost, and never woke up too late to make my breakfast—and yes, *still* with the smoothies. I was annoyed because I felt like my body was the product of my *old* behavior. *I'm fine now! I eat a lot of food!*

One weekend, Sammy came home from college. She stayed the night, ate dinner and breakfast, and hung out with the family. Apparently, in this time, she told my mom that she was worried about me. I imagined them talking in the kitchen after I moved to my room for the night; Sammy telling Mom, in a serious voice, that I was skinnier than the last time she'd been home. This re-stirred the dust of concern that had settled in my mother. Therefore, she brought it up to me, again.

I was infuriated. *Who was Sammy, to just come home one weekend and tell Mom I have an eating disorder? She doesn't even live here most of the time!* I was flustered because, in my mind, I was past questioning whether or not I had a problem—I *was* getting better. I went to my sister's room, where she was typing away on her Macbook, and told her how much I didn't appreciate her bringing the subject back up again.

"That's not even a thing anymore!" I screeched at her, slammed her door, then crawled into bed and muffled my hot tears with a pillow.

CHAPTER 23:

MISUNDERSTANDINGS

The comments I received about my body, for the most part, subsided because it seemed to be a permanent thing—I had retained my skinniness for almost a complete year. I was still so thin that it seemed unacceptable to decline food so, despite my uncanny devotion to "real food," I began to grant myself physical allowance to break my rules for the sake of onlookers. I'd eat a cupcake at the birthday party, plenty of chips and salsa at the Mexican restaurant, and learned to not make a snippy remark when my mom made buttermilk waffles for breakfast.

Of course, I still *preferred* steak and green beans over the equally, if not *less*, caloric-slice of pepperoni pizza, but I had also now learned that I wasn't going to lose all muscle or gain back my double-chin if I let myself slide every once in awhile. I had spent the whole summer and first semester of school eating things that were contaminated with cholesterol and self-imposed sin, and *look*! *I still have my toned body!* I reassured myself. *No worries, I still have control of my life!*

I remember thinking to myself, on multiple occasions: *It's okay if I eat bad, as long as I eat well when I'm at home.*

This hypothesis seemed to work for me, as the times I cooked my own food, or the times that there *was* an option to eat "clean" seemed to outweigh the alternative. When I sat down in the sticky, candy-apple red booth of the local pub with my friends, I knew that, as much as I wanted, I couldn't order a salad. *I'm not that person anymore*, I thought to myself as I scanned the chicken sandwiches. Really, I just didn't want people to think that I was *that* person anymore.

I *did* want to actually gain weight and I was intimately aware of the fact that my body was sickeningly skinny. I just couldn't shake off the peculiar anxiety that flared up when I was around "bad food" and I couldn't escape the fact that eating whole foods and exercising were now the only things that, momentarily, could.

The way some people use drugs, their significant other, hours of Netflix, or faith in a god to feel secure—to give them a sense of comfort in life's messiness—I used food. Healthy food and long runs and my size 0 jeans were the only things that made me feel *okay* for the time being.

I accepted the fact that no one could understand this. I was dismayed when I remembered that people were still under the impression that I had some kind of problem. Every once in awhile, I'd catch myself Google-ing "Why don't I have my period?" or "eating disorder symptoms," or "how to gain weight healthily."

The results presented lists of things that I could relate to myself (hair fallout, lack of energy, perpetual denial) but the words "anorexia" and "bulimia" popped up the most. I couldn't identify myself with their impetuous definitions; bulimia characterized by binging and purging, and anorexia characterized by an avoidance, or lack of hunger for food. I just knew, in all honesty, that I didn't have either. Forcing myself to upchuck my food seemed just as unthinkable as skipping meals and tiny portions did.

I was eating large, healthy portions and since neither of these popularized disorders rang truth for me, I believed that I didn't have a problem. I knew that there were other, broader "eating disorders" but they all seemed blurry and superficial.

I didn't really want to research deeper into them because the mere thought that I may find some accuracy in the results made my whole body squirm. I affirmed that I, Patience Dorman, did not have a disorder. *I just eat healthy,* I reassured myself, *and there's nothing wrong with that.*

I made sure everyone knew that I was self-aware; that I was getting better. I wished I could have added to my speech at the pep assembly, "and, by the way, everyone, I am gaining weight! I do skip workouts and eat bad stuff! I just like the *real* stuff!"—as if this crazy disclaimer absolved me. When people pointed out that there might be something wrong, I wanted to laugh at their "ignorance." *You can't argue with the science—it's an undeniable, research-proven fact that eating whole food is what's best for **everyone**.* I never lost hope that I could gain weight without the refined sugars and artificial flavors.

I valued real food so much that I truly believed pre-packaged foods were the cause of all sickness. Ironically, I became interested in pursuing a career in preventative, holistic healthcare. Despite my creativity, my leadership skills, and my social personality, I wanted to go into the health field because I had myself convinced that food was really the most important thing in the world.

I took speech class and spoke about all the horrible micro-carcinogens in our food, the glory of holistic medicine, and the twisted effect that marketing has on our society.

I still refused to weigh myself and my mom had given up trying. I could tell I was gaining a little bit of weight—a little more softness under my chin, the creases of my abs a little less defined— and that was enough for me. My mother argued that the pace in which I was gaining weight wasn't satisfactory, but I reassured her that I wanted this just as much as she did. "It's not going to take place over night," I fired at her.

My name, Patience, became the perfect title for my journey to re-attain my health. As urgent as I knew recovery was, I didn't just want to gain weight; I wanted to become *normal* with food, and I was convinced that it would be a long, gradual process.

It was the beginning of December and I was still under 115 pounds. My life now seemed to be a configuration of arguments with my mom, with myself, and with the definition of "normal." My affections for friends, family, and potential partners were secondary to my self-improvement formalities. I went to social events only to think, *I'd rather be home*, once I was there.

I was still doing pitiful arm workouts with my 3 lb. weights every morning and I was still avoiding most food groups besides meat, fruits, and vegetables. I was running low on energy and was meandering through life halfheartedly because of my fixation on personal perfectionism.

People's bodies began to be the first thing I noticed about them. As much as I wanted to disregard the way I looked, my innermost thoughts always trickled back to comparison. I judged others the same way I assumed people judged my own rickety body. *Yikes, look at her muffin top—she must be a lazy human being*. Still, most assessments I made were placed on myself.

I subliminally compared myself to girls at student council events, in blogs, at school, and in the gym; *Wow, she has really good calves—note to self: work on calves*. Or *wow, look at her boobs and butt and sexiness—note to self: gain some damn weight*. Most of my *notes to self* were on how to *seem* normal—things I thought I *should* do, but usually failed to reciprocate.

I started, for the first time in all of high school, to revert in an introvert lifestyle. I actually *wanted* to find an excuses to skip barn parties and baseball games so that I could stay in my warm, home-cooked comfort zone. On some Friday nights, I'd work a whole shift at The Fred without eating dinner in hopes that my friends wouldn't have something to do so that I could go home and make myself a meal of spaghetti squash and zucchini.

"Home alone" meant no questions about my weight and no four layers of shirts because I lacked natural insulation. It meant no temptations to share a soft pretzel with a friend and no shameful looks from others. But going home didn't solve the shame I put on myself. It didn't cure my everlasting need to "be better."

Even scarier than the fact that I was a teenager going home to get adequate sleep and nutrients on the weekend, was the fact that this was what I'd come to *prefer*—that *comfort* had become the place in which I sought my happiness.

Christmas came with cookies, candy canes, and caloric celebration. Family events were fun and pleasant until a long lost family member pointed out my weight loss. I participated fully in the gift wrapping and pie baking, but you'd never find any Peppermint Mocha Coffee-Mate polluting my zero-calorie black coffee.

Although the holidays excused indulgence in "unhealthy" foods, even the gifts couldn't rid me of my guilt. It had been almost a year since "The Biggest Loser" and I could sport a jolly grin as I forked down Christmas dinner, but the half cup of stuffing was *still* trickling crumbs across my every thought.

CHAPTER 24:

TOO LITTLE TOO LATE

Despite my pleading, my mom talked to a few professionals about me. One night, she told me that she was planning to schedule an appointment with her friend Paula who was a nutritionist. I pursed my lips in annoyance. She asked me—not *if*—but *when* next Tuesday I would be able to meet with her. I told her I'd look at my schedule and withdrew the thought from my mind.

I had subconsciously planned on coming up with some excuse as to why I wouldn't be able to make it. *I have dance, I don't feel good, I'm out of gas.* I knew, though, that my only valid rebuttal was, *I don't want to go.* I was determined to believe that I didn't have an issue a nutritionist could fix.

I was already gaining weight all by myself, *and besides, it's not like she will tell me I'm **wrong** for saying whole foods are good.* There was no way the professional was going to prescribe me Twinkies and Cheetos three times a day. I was convinced that "Paula" was just going to tell me to do exactly what I was already doing. *I'm better off on my own.*

A week or so went by since the bright "nutritionist" idea was proposed. Then one day, while I was preparing my dinner before I headed off to dance, I got a call from my mom. "Where are you? Did you forget? You have an appointment with the nutritionist... she is here, at The Y, now!"

I had forgotten, or maybe it was just filed away in my huge stash of "thoughts to avoid." Regardless, to say I antagonized the situation would be putting it lightly.

"What?! I can't go! I have dance in 30 minutes and I'm eating dinner and you didn't warn me!" I shouted back. My voice grew higher with every word I said, "No, it's too late, I have dance. We'll have to do it on a different day. Tell her sorry, I can't come." I was trying to enforce the fact that I *couldn't* go—not just that I didn't want to. By the sounds of my outrage, an outsider would have likely thought my mom just informed me that she was sending me to a boarding school for the next two years.

But my mother, now conditioned to my resistance, wasn't going to let me slip this time. After all, the lady was already there, patiently awaiting my arrival. I was furious. I continued to shriek at my mom about how I didn't want and especially didn't *need* to talk to another professional.

My voice cracked on the phone, stimulating a flood of begging sobs. *Don't you remember that I'm making progress?* I wanted to yell. *Don't you see all the effort I've been putting into gaining weight?* I knew she had—I'd reported practically every excess calorie I consumed straight to her. *Did all this prove nothing?* She wasn't giving in, so I shoved down my Mexican salad, grabbed my keys, and drove to The Y, my hands gripping the steering wheel with anger.

I walked into my mom's office, said nothing, and plastered a fake smile on my face as she introduced me to the nutritionist. She was an older woman with curly grey hair and red-framed glasses. "Hi Patience, I'm Paula," she shook my hand warmly. My mom left us alone and we each took a seat in a spinning office chair.

My mother had already explained my situation to Paula and presumably expressed all her worries as well. First, she explained that she typically counsels people who are trying to *lose* weight. *Huh.* I thought. *So you have absolutely no relevancy to me.* Regardless, she asked me questions about my life: what my hobbies are, what

I'm interested in. Slowly, the fury steaming in my head started to lull.

I wanted to make sure she understood how intelligent and self-aware I really was. I gave her the same spiel I told almost anyone who asked: "I joined 'The Biggest Loser,' to hold myself accountable. I went a little overboard on my actions last winter, but since then I've gained weight, seen doctors, and understand how dangerous it all is."

I told her how I was probably just like her in that I saw through all the "healthy" marketing and how I'd learned what's actually *right* to consume. I explained to her how I truly preferred *real* food. *A nutritionist should get that, right?*

We went on to talk about how much everyone's comments and assumptions affected me. It had become the norm for salty tears to roll down my cheeks when I opened up about everything, and this meeting was no exception. Words were spilling out of me faster than my tears and, because I rarely opened up about the topic, it felt liberating. I told her about how alone I felt in my pain. She listened and listened and had a genuine, kind sympathy for me. Paula complimented me and honored me and conversed without judgement.

Then she asked, "What do you think is the worst thing about it all right now?" I thought about it and took a deep breath. We sat in silence for a minute.

"I think it's the fact that my body doesn't align with my words—like my body represents the *old* me and it's so unfair because I feel like that's not who I am anymore!"

Finally Paula concluded, "Well, sweetie, I really want to help you all that I can, but I am just not sure I'm the person for you. I usually help people eat healthier," she apologized. Then she told me that she had a friend who worked in an eating disorder rehab facility whom she could try to contact if I wanted.

Fear glazed my eyes as I smiled and shook my head in consent. Both the phrase "eating disorder" and the word "rehab" shocked my system with sheer panic. I tried to picture myself checking into a recovery center, making friends with all the other other broken-souled teenagers, but my imagination couldn't illustrate the image. The only thing that my mind could conceive were conversations that people around town would have.

"Did you hear, *The Homecoming Queen* is in rehab*?!*"

Paula continued, "I'm not saying you need to go to this place, but maybe she could just kind of get an understanding of where you're at on the eating-disorder spectrum. She could give you some good advice or resources—heck, she could just tell you that you are doing everything right!"

A horrifying thought loitered my mind: *maybe she is right*. Like the hum of a little fly in my ear, I could sense the innermost chambers of my heart craving more out of life. I knew, deep down, the contentment I got from food and exercise were impaired. I was starting to realize that the satisfaction I felt was not coming from joy, but rather a place of security. I knew that if I kept hounding myself about every move I made that I would drill myself all the way down to a cold, hard, rock bottom.

I thought about what kind of food they served in rehab, then it hit me; *maybe this is what I have to do.*

The night after my appointment with Paula, I came and sat next to my mom in her bed. I apologized for going crazy about meeting with the nutritionist and told her what Paula said. "There's this new rehab kind of facility and she said that I could maybe just go and talk to this lady there..." But before I even said three sentences I noticed my mom get sort of squeamish, which made me regret even bringing it up.

Mom's body language proved that she didn't want me to go for the same reason I initially hadn't; she knew I could recover without it. She had seen all I'd accomplished in the past year and knew that, if I set my mind to it, I could gain some weight. I shook the thoughts of "rehab" out of my head, especially when I remembered that my parents would have to spend hundreds of dollars to send me. *I'm not **that** bad.*

I went back into my room and looked at myself in the mirror. I looked into my own eyes and silently scolded myself. *What was I thinking? I don't need some pity facility to fix me. I am capable of myself.* Then I did 100 Russian twists, climbed into my bed, and let subconscious thoughts of hopelessness sneak their way into my dreams.

CHAPTER 25:

WALKING REPERCUSSIONS

I started to really think about what I needed to do to. Mostly, I thought, *how in the hell did this go so far?* My most basic needs were not being met and I was the walking repercussions of it. In addition to daily constipation, I started getting stomach cramps that were, to this day, one of the most painful sensations I've ever experienced.

One day at school, after lunch, the extreme irritation began. I remember vividly picturing my small intestine was getting wrung out beneath my pale skin. The pain was so intense that I wanted to curl up, bawl, and scream all at the same time. I went to the bathroom and called my mom to tell her what was happening. Meanwhile, I clenched my stomach and bit back tears. I was pathetic, but it wasn't going away, so Mom called the school and I went home. I didn't just look sickly skinny, I *felt* sick and tired all the time, too.

I had lost all traces of femininity: my curves, my monthly reminder, and my once prominent craving for boys. I was constantly freezing due to my lack of homeostasis, but I gained some tricks to insulate my bones: wearing leggings under jeans, or long sleeve undershirts (both for warmth and to make it *seem* like I filled out my clothes a little more.)

Years before, I rarely got sick and landed in the "normal" range for every test the doctor administered. The gentle, warm glow that once gleamed off of me was now cold as snow and rigid as ice.

Even stronger than my fear of people looking at my body was a fear of people *touching* my bony body. The once fleshy, tender spirit of my body was replaced by a delicate, porcelain statue that could shatter with the flick of the finger. I wouldn't let my mom rub my back because I knew her fingers would skim my rigid spinal cord. Kisses and hugs were now rarities that I ran from. *I* even started to squirm at my body—the feeling of my fragile hip bones or sharp collarbone in my own two hands sort of unsettled me.

Boys, which were once my life's excitement, didn't strum a single chord of arousal in me. This had something to do with my impaired hormones, but more to do with my own supreme control and self-dependence. I was too consumed with myself and my own schedule to accommodate someone else into it. *There are far more important things to focus on right now.* Relationships, like spirituality, were another thing I tossed to my future "to-do" list.

I was pale, weak, and lifeless; I was collapsing from the inside out. Overall, I'd now regretted ever starting "The Biggest Loser" the year before. I wanted every meal I'd skipped, every pound I'd lost, every strand of hair that fell out, and every conversation I avoided back. I shuffled through my camera roll and appraised my transformations. I wanted to climb through the screen and into my old body.

I now knew, for certain, that unlike my expectations, the grass *wasn't* greener on the other, skinnier side; it was dull and lonely and painful with only small spurts of delightful dopamine. When before, I thought that mastering my body would entrust me with control over my life, it had done the exact opposite.

I wished I would have known that my fantasies about how life would change after losing weight would never come true. I wished I'd known that reaching my "goal body" didn't look and, especially, didn't *feel* the way that Twitter and TV shows and everyone around me seemed to promise it would. I wished I was still my naive self—even if that meant being a little "chubby." I felt like anything would be better than this rut of habits I called life. I'd wished I never started telling myself that I wasn't *enough*. Predominately, I'd wished it wasn't all too late.

CHAPTER 26:

DOCTOR RETRY

After about three weeks of consistent, agonizing stomach aches and more than eight months without a menstrual cycle (that I knew for sure), my mom and I decided that a trip to the doctor was urgent.

This time, walking into the doctor's office was different. The thought of what the doctor would say still conducted horror straight through each fiber of my body, but this time, I knew that backing down wasn't an option. I knew that I couldn't lie about my behavior and I knew that the doc's orders would not be controversial. I knew that, after a year of self-jurisdiction, I needed to believe in the sovereignty of someone else.

On a slushy January day, my mom and I met with the doctor who previously helped heal her broken calcaneus, Doctor Grimsley. His assistant weighed me at 113 pounds, measured me at five foot nine and three-fourths, and led us to his office to wait.

Just as my mom and I started discussing the fact that I was still only 113, the door creaked open and Dr. Grimsley walked in. His smile imitated the color of his lab coat and happy face on the "how do you feel?" poster on the wall. He introduced himself and nestled into his stool.

"Are you taking any medicine?" *No.*

"Do you have any allergies?" *I hope.*

"Are you sure you're not pregnant?" *Ha!*

He then listened politely as my mom explained my "story" and I chimed in with disclaimers. He said that my lack of menstruation was a big deal because it could affect both my fertility and bone density. I shuttered when I realized that my stupid behavior had the potential to wreck my chances of having kids or the stability of my infrastructure.

He recommended that I get some blood tests done and visit a gynecologist to see if it was something anatomical causing the problem. I prayed it was, but he was very honest and said he was fairly certain my problems were derived from my (previous or current) lack of nutrients. His intent was not to just prescribe me some drugs to get my period back or to bulk me up; he wanted to help me.

Then he said, "I think you need to talk to my wife. She's a nutritionist and you are exactly the patient for her." I wanted to roll my eyes, *been there, done that! No help there!*

Somehow, by the end of the appointment, I had a blood test, a bone density test, and a meeting with Dr. Grimsley's wife, Jill, all scheduled for the upcoming week. I had finally put down my armor of resistance—I just wanted it all to be over.

That weekend, my mom and I went to the city to have the tests administered. As we bounced from one facility to the next, I slowly started to realize how much money she was having to spend on everything. *These are the consequences of your actions*, I said to myself. I remember catching a glimpse of the receipt from the radiology clinic in my mom's wallet and feeling queasy—entirely too much of my parents' slim paychecks were being spent on appointments for a problem that *I* infringed on myself.

My mom had been the one harping to me about gaining weight for months, yet *she* was still the one signing the checks. My parents didn't complain about the price, but I recognized how utterly unfair it was, and I swelled with guilt.

CHAPTER 27:

THE PHYSICIAN'S WIFE

A week after the my appointment with Dr. Grimsely, I returned to the doctor's office for my meeting with Jill Grimsely. I still didn't really want to go, but I knew better than to resist. I had to constantly remind myself; *you want this, you want to get better.*

Jill had long, dark hair and compassion seemed to radiate off of her olive-toned skin. Dr. Grimsely introduced us then left us alone. I braced myself—hoped the hour would go by quickly.

Initially, she asked me questions about my job, my friends, my family, my future, what I liked to do. I ranted about my aspirations, making sure my intelligence was evident. She was seemingly impressed and caring about every single embellished aspect of my life that I bellowed about.

We went on to examine my daily intake. I squirmed when I saw her document my glorified recipes and regimens in curly blue ink. I hadn't realized how repetitive and confining my diet was until I was announcing it out loud.

I exaggerated the amount of times I'd eaten oatmeal, and included far too many statements of validation, but I didn't lie to Jill. She explained to me that her purpose wasn't to fix my diet or to get me to gain weight; it was to help me be guilt-free no matter what I was eating. I could tell that, unlike Paula, I was her area of expertise.

We formulated ways that I could be more intentional on upping my caloric intake; another spoon of peanut butter here, a granola bar there. It was surprising and uplifting to me that she wanted to work with what I was *already* doing. I was glad that my distraught notions—that she was going to make me to eat Cocoa Puffs and cinnamon rolls for breakfast—were false. The plan gave me hope; *this is how I get better? Maybe I **can** do this!*

I looked down at my watch to see that it had been almost two hours since the meeting began. I couldn't believe it—I didn't want to leave. Jill's absence of judgement was both miraculous and refreshing to my vulnerable soul.

As we wrapped up, I realized that I'd forgotten she was the wife of my doctor. I'd forgotten that she was a nutritionist. I'd forgotten that I had heavy brick walls covering this part of my life and that, typically, they were paralyzing to dismantle.

Finally, after two and a half hours, I walked out of the office with my new friend's number in my phone, my new diet in hand, and a ridiculous smile on my face.

CHAPTER 28:

THE DAY IT ALL CHANGED

For the next couple of days, I devoted myself to the guidelines that Jill gave me. It felt good to have something to do that I knew was *right*. At the same time, I still felt myself gravitating towards celery over crackers and smoothies over oatmeal. I still felt disappointed when my after-school snack abolished my hunger for dinner.

Although I was no longer going on runs, I still was entertained by "Health and Wellness" podcasts streaming through my ears. Two days after the appointment, I was weight lifting and listening to one of my favorite health-promoting podcasters. The episode was on micro and macro nutrients and how vital it is to pay attention to them.

As I moved on to squats, I thought about Jill. *Would she approve of me listening to this podcast?* Then, unconsciously—as if I couldn't control the movement of my skinny fingers—I typed "eating disorder" into the little podcast search box. *Enter.* Without even reading the description, I clicked the first episode that appeared. Right then and there — during my third set of squats—the world as I knew it completely flipped around.

PART II:

FACING MY FEARS

CHAPTER 29:

"WHEN WE DENY OUR STORIES, THEY DEFINE US. WHEN WE OWN OUR STORIES, WE GET TO WRITE THE ENDING."

- BRENÉ BROWN, *Rising Strong*[2]

The podcast I'd found was hosted by a woman with a balmy, impassioned voice. She introduced herself as Maddy Moon and spoke of her obsessive "clean-eating," fitness-model background and how she had since turned "sane."[3] She talked about her internal conflicts as she strived to meet society's expectations. Then, she talked about the climactic moments when she realized how miserable she was in life.

Maddy Moon realized that her tan, sculpted, award-winning body had turned into the radical antagonist to her former fantasies. As I listened attentively to the first episode, my breath was practically taken from me with every new sentence she said. *Holy shit*, I thought. *That's exactly how I*

2 Brown, B. (2015). Rising Strong. New York: Random House.

3 Podcast - Maddy Moon. (n.d.). Retrieved May 15, 2016, from http:// maddymoon.com/show/

feel. Other people have had the exact same feelings as me!?

When I came home that night, I feverishly listened to every episode on the channel. I was captivated by the compatibilities that I had with Maddy and every single guest she had on her show. They *too* dealt had problems and looked to their bodies, restriction, and food for security. They *too* became obsessed with real, whole foods and had a relentless, disgraceful inner-critic. They *too* lacked energy and passion and periods. They *too* endured social and emotional sacrifices for the sake of their own "health."

Most amazing of all, they spoke of all of these things as if they were *okay*. They didn't deny or try to hide the the fact that they had been the agitators of their own unhappiness. They were rejoicing in humility.

As the week continued, there was rarely a moment that I wasn't listening to one of Maddy's podcasts, reading a blogpost, or discovering more about this self-loving, soul-healing community which, before, I didn't even know existed. I ached for the self-acceptance and was in awe of the courage of the people in the podcasts, blogs, and videos.

Their words about their previous, "healthy" lives seemed to depict me seamlessly; like all podcasters and bloggers made a criminal plan to sneak into my brain and steal my deepest thoughts. I couldn't fathom the amount of truth I found in their insight.

I had finally found the word that described what I, and so many other women, had. And most telling, I was right about not having a popularized eating disorder; it was called "orthorexia." A quick search of the term was like a memoir of my life for the past year; every symptom, story, and syntax aligning perfectly to myself. Its most basic, dry definition read, "Or·tho·rex·i·a, *noun,* an obsession with eating foods that one *considers* healthy." [4] This diagnoses fit me unlike any of my clothes did; frighteningly well.

As I absorbed story after story of the flawed lives of others, I started to realize things about *my own* life. All my neurotic, subconscious behavior was floating into my awareness. I was starting to see that I had this extreme discernment way longer than I'd originally thought—it didn't just begin when I won "The Biggest Loser," it had been accumulating my whole life.

[4] Google. (n.d.). Retrieved May 09, 2016, from https:// www.google.com/webhp?sourceid=chrome-instant

I remember Maddy Moon preaching in one episode, "What if you died tomorrow? Eating a spinach salad or tofu or the *right* amount of protein isn't going to lower your chances of getting hit by a bus."

Her words thrashed something in the deepest cavity of my heart, like this concept wasn't just common knowledge but was wisdom I was dying to hear. *Woah,* was all I could think. *If I died tomorrow, would I be glad that I spent it avoiding milkshakes and hugs and friendships? If I died tomorrow, would I still be spending it piddly lifting weights and making paleo pancakes?*

It was like all of the cliche phrases about "taking life for granted" finally clicked. It was a colossal awakening of my own mind. As Maddy continued to ask rhetorical questions, I searched for the answers in the context of my own life.

"What's making you feel like you need control? What is your *actual* purpose in life?" Epiphanies flared up like book pages in the quickening wind; *I am so much more than what I look like.*

I dug and dug deeper into myself and found things that had been secluded in oblivion for the past three years. *My friends, my family—everyone*

*—they do not love me because of **my body**. They could care less!* Every single thing that I'd adhered my beliefs to were proved fallacious.

My interest, emotions, and outlook were provoked. I started to jot down notes, afraid that I would lose the holy wisdom I was hearing. "Your body is not your masterpiece, your life is," and "Trust your own sense of self," and "What is the one thing you can do where thoughts of food, anxiety, and evil cease to exist?"

Answers arose from my neglected intuition. Art and friendship and leadership and helping and writing and family—*those* were the things I wanted to pursue! Not micro-nutrients and six-packs and vegan recipes. I was overwhelmed by these revelations and was eagerly inspired to implement all that I had learned into my life.

The first thing I did (as recommended by a podcaster) was to rid myself of all the things in my life that weren't serving my happiness; things that fed into my pursuit of security instead of helping me face my prevalent fear of the unknown. On Instagram, I unfollowed every supermodel, reality

TV star, and every other gorgeous person whom I only knew by their username. I un-saved every podcast channel that related to "health." I revived with a new art project so that I could redirect my attention when my mind wandered toward food.

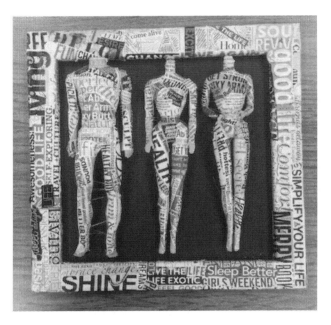

I began to realize how absurd the consensus on women's bodies in our society is—how universal phrases like "I'm so fat," and "look at you, eating a salad, you're so *healthy*," are. My younger self placed so much value on my figure because a thin body was the constant undercurrent to the messages society taught me. I always wanted to *better* myself and couldn't comprehend that I didn't have to.

I looked up "body-acceptance" videos on Youtube and deliberately made my mind soak up their messages. Through a blog, I found a Facebook page of other women (and a few men) who were going through the exact same journeys to recovery as I was. It was mind-boggling to see the amount of understanding that everyone had for each other and the encouragement that was enabled because of it. In the matter of a few days, the excitement of these new communities—of the fact that I wasn't *alone*—and of the self-awareness I was developing, was beginning to fill the void that my life had become. I couldn't get enough.

I told my mom about my renewed mindset and her response was less than promising. She was taken back by my jubilation but didn't mask her weariness. "I'll believe it when I see it," she said. A smirk formed on my mouth, *you just wait*, I thought.

I was starting to understand what needed to be done in order for my deep wrinkles of struggle to smooth out. Scribbled words of inspiration and self-reflection journal entries were propitious, but I knew that those things alone weren't going to fix the problem. I was going to have to implement my forsaken fears into my everyday life. Despite the appeal that I felt towards the infamous phrase "face your fears," it proved to be no reviving, uplifting task.

The phrase I'd heard of repetitively was "intuitive eating." Its name describes its premise; our bodies always *know* what they need to consume and we must abide to this by not challenging our intuition. I pictured myself in a college cafeteria, an abundance of options before me, and stopping to ask, *what are you hungry for, Body?* It seemed unfeasible, like a dream that I my all-too-common panic would obliterate.

Intuitive eating made sense to me, as my body had given me a million clues of it's misery, but *actually* allowing myself to eat *all* types of foods ignited fear in me. Regardless, I was determined. I remember walking into my kitchen and making myself think, *what if I could eat anything I wanted?*

The idea that the French baguette on the counter and the artificially-flavored raspberry preserves in the fridge were now acceptable to consume was both exciting and scary.

CHAPTER 30:

A TASTE OF FREEDOM

One night, I came home from a long night at work, still hungry from my small, rushed dinner of leftovers from The Fred. As if it was a sign from the universe, I opened our fridge to see that my grandma had left a pan of homemade mac and cheese right in front of the broccoli. In about a minute, I had a plate of the golden elbows in the microwave, saliva building in my mouth, and an idiot grin on my face. I looked at my reflection on the shiny black door. *I'm really doing this.*

My mom was in the family room talking with our neighbor. I took the warm plate, grabbed a spoon, and headed out to join them in their gossip. As I was leaving the kitchen, I caught a whiff of butter steaming off the macaroni and looked down at the dish in my hands. *Wait, are you sure you're hungry?* And, *is this really what you're hungry for?*

Everything in me knew the right answer, and it was liberating to actually admit that; *yes!* Then I walked into the family room and ate my mac and cheese without one second thought. I ate it, piece by piece, and let myself blissfully drift into the cheesy, childhood taste that it brought back to me. It was the first time in a long, long time that I enjoyed eating pasta—maybe enjoyed eating *anything*—without focusing on the backlash I'd later grant myself.

As my mom and our neighbor talked and I munched away, I noticed my mom's glance trickle to me and my snack. I knew she couldn't believe that I had willingly chosen *macaroni* to eat. It filled me with with an alien feeling of self-pride.

My neighbor likely didn't even see the significance that moment entailed, but for me, it was huge. I wasn't eating the macaroni because I felt like I had to, because my mom was watching, or because I needed to gain weight—I was eating it because I really, truly wanted to.

Before that night in my family room, I don't believe I had ever in my life known what it felt like to be present with food. After I had cleared my plate, I was satiated. I was no longer hungry, I was not exceedingly full, and I wasn't thinking about how the carbs might *kill* me. The macaroni had been just enough; I was ready to put my plate in the dishwasher and move on with my night.

I brushed my teeth, changed into my pajamas and, and, for the first time in months, didn't do an ab work-out before crawling into bed. The feelings of freedom I'd gained that night were more delicious than anything I'd ever tasted.

Soon, it was time for my second meeting with Jill. I was eager to tell her about my life-changing epiphanies and as we sat down, I told her to brace herself; I was going to spurt a lot on her at once. I wanted to tell her, *well, I've basically turned into a new person since the last time we talked*, but didn't want to seem over-ambitious.

"I realized that it was never about food," I told her, "it was about a sense of control." Saying this out loud felt like I was unshackling chains that were entwined around me. I told her about Maddy Moon and the macaroni and the art project. I read her the notes I had jotted down and the definition of "orthorexia." I confessed how I learned, from the vulnerabilities of others, that I was seeking control from my body; how I realized that food is simply *fuel* and that the purpose of life was not to obsess over it.

I rambled on, "It's like, we claim things as 'good' or 'healthy,' but when we stop and think about it, there is nothing inherently *bad* about a PB&J. *We* are the ones pasting these labels onto innocent, inanimate objects like food! I don't know what happened, it just hit me—why would would I let a damn *sandwich* harbor precious space in my creative, passionate, purposeful head?!"

I was beaming with zeal and she was dumbfounded. As I continued, Jill just smiled and shook her head in disbelief. It had to have been thirty minutes before she got a peep in.

For the next hour, we talked about everything from intuitive eating to body-image to lifelong reflections. She helped me rummage through my memories to find the roots of my eating disorder and my fear of uncertainty.

I left the office feeling prideful, placid, and pining to experience life through this new perspective. Jill was no longer my nutritionist; she was exclusively *my* person. *My* person whom I could tell anything to and who completely understood. *My* person that listened and *actually cared* about every part of my sputtery, perplexing, two-hour rambles.

I wanted to skip to my car and shout out to the world about how *free* I felt. On the car ride home, I rolled down my windows and screamed every single word to the obnoxious pop song playing from my radio. I felt extraordinarily euphoric.

For the next couple of weeks, opportunities to confront my fears seemed to arise all around me. One Sunday morning at work, the chef asked me if

I wanted to split a hamburger with him. It was like some god was saying, *boom! Here ya go. Are you sure you can do this?*

Casually, I replied, "I'd love to share a burger." I hadn't had a hamburger—at least a hamburger *and* a bun—for years, and the thought of it made my stomach grumble with appetite. He handed me the sandwich, oozing with red juice and greasy residue, and I didn't feel panicked. As I lifted the sandwich to my mouth, I realized how wondrous it was that I hadn't summoned an excuse as to why I didn't *need* half of a hamburger. *I'm a freaking badass.*

To this day, I don't think I've ever tasted anything quite as good as the mouth-watering flavors that the burger, and my lack of self-deprivation, delivered. The moment felt so empowering and and life-altering that I snapped a picture of it. I never wanted to forget the way that silly little moment made me feel.

And so I embarked on my journey of extreme self-therapy. I continued to choose foods that I knew would have been forbidden just a month before. Nutella and muffins and non-"low-fat" yogurt presented new, exciting provocations. I signed up for a 10-day program called "The F-it Diet" that encouraged, inspired, and wrenched my heart of its truth via email.[5] The emails asked me questions that probed areas of my life that I had, before, avoided confrontation with.

I remember one of them, day #8, asking me "What are you the most scared of? What is the reason you keep yourself small and safe? What are you protecting yourself from?"

No matter how much homework I had to complete, silverware I had to buff, or notifications I had to check, I would physically force myself to put away my phone, get out a piece of paper, and write out my answers. I stared at the blank page for a solid two minutes, questioning whether *sugar* and *diabetes* were appropriate answers. Then it came to me. I wrote *anxiety* down on the paper.

Then, like the ballpoint pen had a mind of its own, a whole page of words seemed to pour out of me. *Rejection. Imperfection. Oblivion. Failure. Judgement. Humiliation. Vulnerability.* I looked at the list and realized how subjective, how

---

[5]Caroline Dooner's "The Fuck It Diet" - thefuckitdiet.com

narcissistic, and yet, how vastly ubiquitous all my "fears" were.

I realized that I *did*, in fact, have fears. I realized that, no matter how hard I tried, I would never be indestructible, flawless, or in control of my life—and neither would anyone else! *What a radical, liberating concept.* It was as if seeing these words in real, tangible form released the tight strain around my trachea. I could finally breath.

CHAPTER 31:

PLEASURE WITHOUT JUSTIFICATION

The next month I gained a new love for life. My favorite part of the week began to be Wednesday afternoons when I met with Jill and we delved into every intimate detail of my life. She weighed me every meeting, but she wouldn't tell me what the number was. The blind-weighings were Jill's way of ensuring my progress, and *my* way of learning that the number on the scale *meant absolutely nothing*. Our friendship grew as did the skinny jeans around my waist—tighter with every week.

I quit exercising, quit pre-packing my lunches, and quit wasting my time studying nutrition facts and "healthy" recipes. I was afraid these things might trigger the intrapersonal jurisdiction that was once so prevalent. I thought about how much energy, time, and worry I handed over to my body and food. I dreamed about how great my life was going to be when I spent that time crafting genuine relationships, doing artwork, and serving others; things I *actually* cared about.

When I felt my mind meandering through thoughts like, *what should I have for dinner?* Or, *wow, I'm SO full,* I tried to redirect my attention to things like, *how can I reach out to someone else right now? How can I be more compassionate towards myself?*

But, as sweet as it sounds, my disposition didn't just crumble away like a piece of cake. In fact, my road to recovery was *far* from being "a piece of cake." In times when I felt bored, flustered, or the tiniest bit stressed, I felt myself gravitate toward old behavior. When I was mad because Mille stole my new dress, because someone commented on how skinny I *still* was, or because I had four writing assignments due in one week, I felt my itch to control inflame.

I sensed the part of me wanting to reach for the skim milk over the half-and-half. I felt my hand gravitate toward the hem of my shirt when I looked in the mirror…

But right then, I'd shut myself up. I'd tell my inner-critic, *not today, bitch!*

I *made* myself not lift up my shirt—I didn't want to get any satisfaction from the fact that, despite it's expanding, I still had a crease down the center of my stomach. *A toned stomach proves nothing*, I reminded myself. I hadn't abolished my humanistic yearn for comfort, but I became aware of the fact that I couldn't run from it; that my only choice was to accept it.

On my eighteenth birthday, after much contemplation, (*how will I bring up the subject? How I will phrase everything?*) I opened up to Emma about how I felt my life had radically changed in a month. It had become my new favorite topic of conversation and my only topic of thought.

In the past year, hostility and snippy comments were regularities to our lifelong friendship. My weight loss, my fixation on achievement, and my uncanny maturation caused a discrete loophole in our tight bond.

I told her about Jill, Maddy Moon, and my process of healing. I came clean to her about how sorry I was for being the force that weakened our friendship. She was surprised that I was finally talking about my weight—that I was admitting I didn't have it all together.

My words had dissolved the discomfort that we both had, which had been restricting our relationship from reaching its full potential. That conversation restored the strength in our friendship that we had started to lose sight of.

PART III:

FAITH

CHAPTER 32:

THE BLUE PT CRUISER

Towards the end of February, I was driving to the city with my grandma for a super belated birthday lunch. My grandmother is the most biblically speaking, Christian-claiming person I know. Every conversation we had would relate back to God and, as much as I wanted to roll my eyes, I'd figured out how to make it look like I was entertained.

I accepted the fact that "Jesus talk" was just a part of who my grandma was, and that none of it would ever *really* resonate with me for more than five minutes. "I pray for you, everyday. You know that, right Patience?" she'd say.

As we drove down the highway, we talked about politics, school, our family, and more—every conversation ending with something about The Lord, naturally. As I thought about what exciting new food I would try for lunch, I haphazardly listened to what she way saying.

Then, I'm not sure if it was something she said or simply a feeling from my gut, but suddenly, my attention was caught. It was as if the dial to my own, selfish thoughts was turned down and I could *actually* hear what my grandma was saying to me.

I saw, for the first time, how every note of her voice and every cell in her body sweltered with belief. I leaned back in my seat, bewildered by this phenomenon I was witnessing. As we kept talking, and as she brought every story back to God, I strangely started to embrace her manner. It was as though my face had been splashed with a sudden, freezing cold *understanding*.

My eyes were opened to how much my grandma truly, deeply believed in this higher power and I, finally—for the first time in my whole life—understood *why*. Sitting in my grandma's blue PT Cruiser, listening to a Christian rock radio station, I recognized the beauty and greatness to having faith.

Like Haley Watson had said to me two years before; if nothing else, you can surely feel how *good* it feels to have somewhere to rest your beliefs. It was like, in that very moment, every tacky tattoo and hand-painted calligraphy of the word "faith" suddenly made sense. *Having faith in God means admitting that I am not in control and admitting that HE is!* As we arrived at the restaurant and the waitress handed us the menus, my mind thudded with this revelation.

CHAPTER 33:

"ONLY IN A WORLD WHERE FAITH IS DIFFICULT CAN FAITH EXIST."

- LEE STROBEL, *A CASE FOR CHRIST*

More significant than anything I learned from self-love mantras or the body-acceptance community was the truth of why I was unsatisfied with my life; I was striving to gain authority of my life even though something—*someone*—much greater than me was already in absolute control of it. It was life-altering.

I felt like I'd finally found the answers to my problems, the solvent to my anxiety, the *purpose* to religion that I could never quite comprehend. *Why would I worry if God already has my life planned out?* I opened my mind up to the idea that maybe, just maybe, all my fears were simply the outcome of my disbelief—of my lack-of-faith.

For the next couple of weeks, I let that car ride with my grandma sink in. I let my mind render on the thought that my revelations about Christ and his ownership of my life were very likely the truth. The thoughts resided in the back of my skull—in the tiny sutures that hold typically-forgotten information. But after the mention of "church" by a friend, or in the cozy, secluded moments before I closed my eyes to rest, the thoughts would return.

Finally, one Wednesday afternoon, as our meeting neared its end, Jill asked me if there was anything else on my mind. "Anything, at all, that you want to get off of your chest?"

I tapped my finger on the desk, trying to think about what I could say to extend the duration of the meeting—to keep the special moment alive. Then it came to me; I told Jill about the flash of discovery I'd had in the car with my grandma. I admitted the doubts I had in God, or maybe, just the distaste I had for everyone's question-less and seemingly over-joyous endorsement of Him.

Jill's response seemed to validate that I had made the right choice; that my intuition was in no way, a liar when it told me to tell her about that car ride. She said, "I know this sounds crazy, but I was praying about this in the car *today*. I was asking God if he wanted me to open up to you about this, and what you just said to me proves that I can—proves that I *should*."

I was confused. I didn't know what she would say. *How were my words a sign?* I was afraid that she was going to whip out her Bible and start counseling me through its passages. I didn't want that to happen. I knew that if she started preaching to me about God that. Despite my new interest in the subject, I would feel compelled to go along with it. Thus, the authenticity of our friendship, which I so-dearly valued, would be lost.

But Jill did nothing of the sort. Her answer proved, yet again, that my worries were irrational and pointless. Instead, that sunny Wednesday afternoon, was the day that I learned why Jill and I got along so well...

She told me that she, *too* had struggled with disordered eating. She told me that from a young age, through high school, college, and a good chunk of her adulthood, she shared the same agony and search for comfort as I had.

Jill and I were such a good match because she had something that no one else had; despite my doctor's, Mom's, teachers', and Paula's copious amounts of sympathy, Jill had something much more promising: empathy.

As I was just starting to get a grasp of how powerful this similarity was—how I would have *never* guessed this—Jill continued with her story. She went on to explain how she knew, for certain, that she would have never healed without developing faith in God. She admitted that *she too* once doubted Christianity, for all of the same reasons that I had.

Then, she told me about *her* eye-opening, belief-igniting moment; the time that she, by accident, picked up a book called "The Case for Christ" from her in-law's shelf and decided to give it a read.[6] Similar to my moment in the car with my grandma, Jill's whole perspective changed the moment she opened the book.

Now, both of our secrets were out. Any undermining fears of judgment or incorrect timing were shattered. She opened up about how it was often difficult for her to help clients recover without mentioning Faith. This was because she truly felt like it was Jesus who restored her and eradicated her need to control, restrict, and perfect. Strangely, everything she was saying made perfect sense to me.

---

[6] Strobel, L. (1998). The case for Christ: A journalist's personal investigation of the evidence for Jesus. Grand Rapids, MI: Zondervan.

I knew her testimony wasn't some claim for innocence, validation, or forgiveness. I knew the reason every word she was said seemed to enclose my heart and soul and I knew the reason I no longer cared if someone walked into the office and heard us talking about Jesus: God had saved me.

CHAPTER 34:

SEEK AND YOU SHALL FIND

Because of Jill, I adopted the thought that maybe, *just maybe*, my disordered eating was now subsiding because God had planned it to. This acceptance was pivotal; I was eager to learn more about these unfamiliar feelings of Faith I had tugging at me. Jill let me borrow "A Case for Christ" and I read it thoroughly, digesting it's legitimate, non-fluffy evidence that God *has* to exist.

As I flipped through the pages, every paragraph contradicted all the ignorant conceptions I had about Christianity that I was always too scared to say aloud. The author is a former atheist and I appreciated the lack of embellishment in his findings. He put God in relative terms and even blatantly said that it's not real Faith if there is no doubt present; *No! It's not feasible to walk on water or arise from the dead! That is why they are miracles!* **That** *is why He is God!* It was reassuring to know that I didn't have to pretend like I had some righteous, certain ideology about Jesus.

My pea-sized notions were snowballing in my stomach, and eventually, they grew large enough to make me desire the attainment of strong, sincere beliefs. I prayed to God about how I wanted to strengthen my relationship with him. I wrote down concepts that I didn't quite get so that I could ask Jill about them in our next meeting. I reconnected with long lost friends whom I knew regularly praised His spirit. I was swimming out of the lukewarm, socially-motivated beliefs I'd been drowning in for so long.

Jill and I continued to meet weekly, and, as my anxiety with food calmed, conversations about Faith started to take up the bulk of our meetings. She helped me see that God had put me through my eating disorder for a *reason*. She helped me comprehend that nothing—not our encounter, not my loss of a period, not my stumbling across Maddy Moon—happened by chance. God had every single second of it planned before I was even *alive*.

It hit me that I was put through my agonizing journey because it gave me a deep appreciation for my body, food, and relationships, no matter what their form. It gave me a whole new level of empathy and passion in helping others with similar struggles. It gave me a story, an inferno to ignite my creativity. It gave me relief from all anxiety and worries.

I would have never established a relationship with God had I not endured my eating disorder and that filled—and continues to fill—me with a baffling gratitude. I realized that, through pain, I was given the greatest gift of all; I was given Faith.

CHAPTER 35:

PRESENT

It's around two in the afternoon and I'm sitting in a coffee shop, writing in my sticker-collaged laptop, and sipping warmish coffee from a ceramic mug. I look up from my work and watch the dynamic characters of the city pass by the big window in front of me. I stretch my legs onto the seat in front of me and notice a new, shallow dimple of cellulite where my thigh is squished against the seat. Then, I hear my stomach grumble and I think, *thanks God for the signal!*

Despite the large amount of editing I still have to accomplish, the texture I just found on my thigh, and the fact that it's technically past lunch time, I stand up and head to the register to get some food.

I take a look at the menu, equipped with mediterranean salads, chicken kabobs, and spanakopita. It all looks deliciously enticing. The man behind the counter looks strikingly Greek with his tan skin and dark mustache. With a thick, velvety accent, he asks me what I would like to eat.

I glance at the menu again and remind myself that I can have *anything* I want. I search my intuition, which I have become a lot better at, but eventually give up. "What's your most popular dish?" He answers in two seconds, the gyro. "I'll take that," I say without a hint of hesitation. I fetch eight dollars from my wallet and feel no connection to the meaningless, dingy paper I place in his hand.

As I wait for my food, the revelation of the moment sinks in and I feel a sweet, calm harmony wash over me. After a few minutes, the Greek barista calls my name, I pick up my food, and head back to my secluded little workspace. I find the spot I left off in my writing, nestle into my chair, and take a bite of my gyro. The warm lamb meat and the tang of the Tzatziki excite my taste buds. I continue to write, swallowing a chunk of the sandwich after every other sentence or so. I can feel the authentic, flavorful food suppressing my hunger with each luscious bite I take.

With only one small bite left, I realize that I am full and set the scraps down on the plate. I refocus my attention on my computer and write. Eventually, my eyes trickle over to the pita bread still sitting on the plate. Just six months before, that little piece of bread would have obstructed my creativity, evoked my anxiety, and threatened my existence, but now, I have peace. *Look at how far you've come*. I lean back in the cozy chair, feeling blissfully triumphant with myself and the magnitude of this accomplishment.

I listen to see if my inner-critic will storm in, but she doesn't—I don't wish I would've chosen something else from the menu and I don't lose any dignity by dining alone. I don't question the food's nutritional value and I'm not affected by the cellulite I found on my leg. Sitting in my nook of the cafe, I feel solidarity confident.

The table next to me is filled with college-aged girls and an older mentor that must have come to visit them. I accidentally listen to their joyous conversations and I smile, thinking about how gratifying it will be to reunite with my family and friends after a semester away at college. I turn back to my computer, then reach into my backpack to grab a pen. My hand skims the smooth leather of my new Bible that Jill gifted me for graduation—a reminder of His presence in that very moment.

I hesitate, then, amidst the strangers in the coffee shop, I close my eyes and pray. My lips move but my words aren't audible. I thank God for redeeming my life; for letting me be at ease as I eat, as I sit alone, and as I submit my story to the screen of my computer. I thank God for healing me and for providing me with a complete, wholehearted understanding of His word—something I never had before. I think about the transformation of my life and I rejoice. I ask God to help me continue to find my happiness in Him, and Him only—not through my body, my achievements, others, or myself.

As I finish up, I don't look around to see if anyone sees me, I don't lack the words to finish my prayer, and I don't stumble over the word "Amen." My hands unlock and dwindle back to their places on the keyboard. Then, with God whispering through my soul, I pour my heart onto the page in front of me.

I catch my glowing reflection in the shiny screen of my laptop and realize that I've finally seized the feelings I'd been chasing my whole life. Sitting by myself in the corner of this little coffee shop, I—finally—feel completely, unquestionably, content.

ACKNOWLEDGEMENTS:

I AM INDEBTED IN THANK YOU'S:

I, first and foremost, must thank my mom for putting up with me throughout every single "phase" of my life. You intimately experienced my wrath of denial and thirst for control yet, miraculously, you never lacked hope for your daughter. Thanks for still loving me despite my abundance of snippy comments, my obsession with myself, and my over-ambitious aspirations. I know I wasn't the easiest crayon to sharpen, but somehow you still did. I'll forever be thankful that you (and Dad) formed me into the creative spirit I am today.

Thank you Dad for always buying me cookies when I wanted them, grilled chicken when I wanted that, and for supporting no matter what phase I'm in. Thanks for showing me that a man's love should never be contingent on the condition of a woman's body.

Thank you Jill Granneman for being the angel that saved me; for being my personal outlet to God when I needed salvation the most. I will cherish our conversations and friendship for the rest of my life. I will (continue to) rejoice in gratitude to God for sending you my direction.

Thanks Sammy for being my lifelong role model and for showing me what true kindness and integrity looks like. Also, thanks for blessing this book with *your* outstanding talent and creating the cover artwork in a ridiculously short time frame. I don't know who I'd be without you.

Thanks Mille for always giving me the amount of humility I needed. Thanks for always providing the cold smack in the face of "It's not like you'll eat that anyways!" I deserved every bit of it.

Thank you Emma Goff for always listening when I rant about myself, especially when I don't even reciprocate the favor. Thanks for being the most positive light in my life and for sticking by my side the past 9 years—that's a lot of phases! You're the best friend I could ever ask for and I still don't understand how I got so lucky to take part in such a genuine relationship.

Thanks Zac Ruffolo for being the person I can truly tell anything to and who always genuinely cares. I can't express how amazing it feels to know that I have someone who always thinks on the same wavelength as me and whom I know will never judge me. Thanks, also, for being a grammar god and helping me with the part of writing that I'm not fan of.

Thanks to Haley Watson and Bryce Fuemmeler—you guys are two of the most inspiring, intelligent young persons I've ever gotten the chance to be friends with. I owe you a plethora of artwork and homemade desserts for editing this book. You guys were the first-hand witnesses to the gore and rawness of this novel, so thanks for crossing my t's, dotting my i's and supporting me in the process. I know it wasn't an easy task.

Thanks to all of my friends whom never seemed to care what I looked like; you validated that I am not valued for my looks. I love you all so much (reference chapter 21).

Thanks to all of my teachers for being so compassionate to me, especially those who had the initiative to express their concerns. (Also, thanks for letting me disregard class work to write this book!)

Thanks Grandma Dede, for always reminding me about Jesus, even when I didn't act amused. I am now remarkably aware of God's glory and work in my life, so I guess it all paid off!

Lastly, thanks to Maddy Moon, Caroline Dooner, Brené Brown, and Andie Mitchell for being the ultimate inspiration for this book. Maddy Moon, you taught me that I am not alone. Caroline Dooner, you taught me to accept and conquer my fears. Brené Brown, you taught the divine power of vulnerability, and Andie Mitchell, you taught me that my story *is* important to tell.

Thanks to everyone who has placed their fingerprints on the watercolor painting of my life. My heart overflows with appreciation, admiration, and gratitude for every single one of you. Thanks to every person who picked up this novel and took time to give it a read. I hope my story resonated somewhere in your soul, body, or spirituality. I hope you know that God's plan for you has nothing to do with the way you look; that you are worth so much more than your inner-critic is probably telling you. Use this book as your personal reminder that there is SO much more in life than appearances and achievement—you just have to open your eyes.

Overall, I would not be the Patience I am today without the unfathomable amount of patience you all had with me—*sorry, had to*. Let this story express my thankfulness and my actions reflect my authenticity.

Made in the USA
Columbia, SC
18 June 2018